hello

First of all, thanks for picking up this book. It contains the story of how we set up and have been running innocent, and the things we've learnt from doing so. Our mistakes, lessons and bright ideas are all in here, to help anyone wanting to start their own business or accelerate their existing one. The theory is to avoid the things we got wrong and maybe use some of the things we got right (and hopefully not the other way round).

It's been ten years since we, as a group of three friends, sold our first smoothies from a stall at a music festival in west London. Over that period, the business has grown to have a turnover of more than £100 million and our drinks are now sold in over 8000 outlets across 13 different countries in Europe. We can honestly say it has been the hardest thing we have ever done – we faced rejection from the whole investment community and the entire food and drink industry. It has taken its toll emotionally, physically and personally. There have been periods of hot sweaty panic, despondency and sheer exhaustion.

But no matter how tough it's been, no matter how many times we've been told 'no' and 'it won't work', not for one second has any of us regretted that moment in August 1998 when we resigned from our jobs to set up innocent full time. Since that moment it has been, and continues to be, the most exhilarating, life-enhancing ride, and we're extremely grateful to all the people – drinkers, retailers, suppliers and team members – who help make innocent possible.

If you're thinking of setting up your own business, we couldn't recommend it highly enough.

And hopefully, in some small way, this book will help.

Good luck.

contents

chapter one
what's the big idea?

What's the big idea?

It's difficult to know whether entrepreneurs are born or made, but each of us showed signs of having entrepreneurship in our blood from an early age. By age 11 we were all separately embarking on our first 'business' ventures: Adam was doing his classmates' Maths homework in return for cash, Jon was in detention for selling bangers and cigarette lighters he'd acquired on a day trip to Calais, and Richard had a nice sideline trading Smurf stickers.

This common entrepreneurial trait was something we discovered when we first met at university, bonding over a shared desire to improve the night life options in Cambridge, which at that time was not going to be difficult. Asking around, we knew there were people (like us) that wanted an alternative to drinking beer and singing rugby songs in the college bar. So we decided to start organising dance events.

Between the three of us there was a clear division of labour: Adam and Richard would DJ and promote the nights; and Jon, the only person in the college with a computer in his room, would design the flyers and posters.

We had the most fun with a fortnightly house night called 'Please', which became so popular the college authorities eventually shut it down. Still, we got to keep the decks in our room, and it allowed us to offer budding female DJs late-night 'DJ lessons' back at our place.

The success of 'Please' taught us several things:

1. Where there's an unmet need, there's an opportunity

2. It was possible to start something successful from scratch with no experience

3. We enjoyed working together and made a good team

4. The 'DJ lessons' tactic didn't work; back in our rooms, the name 'Please' became all too appropriate

Those first three points really resonated with us, and came to form the basis of a conversation that we would have many times over the coming years; namely, wouldn't it be great if one day we set up a business together?

Certainly, the idea of avoiding a regular job appealed. But when college ended, we found ourselves taking the safer option of going to work in established companies. Adam went to McKinsey, the management consultancy, and then Virgin Cola; Jon chose Bain, another consultancy, and Richard went into advertising. Throughout these early years, we continued to share houses, meet for drinks most weekends and go on holidays with each other. And one thing remained constant: the conversation about wanting to set up a business together.

Four years later, driving through Switzerland to the resort of Davos for a snowboarding weekend, the topic was raised yet again. One of us said simply, 'We either have to stop talking about this, or get on with it, otherwise we'll drive ourselves nuts.' So on that trip we made a simple commitment to each other: by the end of the weekend either we would come up with a business idea that we were excited by, or we would drop the topic for good.

Follow the need

To come up with an idea, we looked for areas where we could identify a problem, and then solve it; to 'follow the need' as we now call it. And we wanted something we could be proud of, something in addition to the pursuit of money. So we set ourselves the challenge of coming up with an idea that would make life a little bit better and a little bit easier. A thought that played to both our altruistic and our lazy sides.

The first idea that we came up with was 'the amazing Electric Bath'. It scored points for originality, if nothing else. This was a bath that would fill itself to a pre-designated temperature and pre-designated level all at the touch of a button. Bath time would be revolutionised. As the marketing guy, Richard was excited about the consumer benefit: *no more water that was too hot or cold, no more baths that overflowed.* As the commercial guy, Adam was excited about the size of the market: *we could sell it into hotel chains around the world.* But it was Jon, the one who had done the degree in engineering at Cambridge, who was really champing at the bit; this was the perfect opportunity to validate his geeky degree course, and he enthusiastically outlined complicated plans of how the bath would work.

Later on that evening, over beers in a bar, it finally dawned on us that we had missed a small design flaw – the central idea featured water and electricity in close proximity to each other. Rather than make life easier and better for people, we were likely to be making their lives shorter. Not good.

And even if we got over the electrocution issue, we weren't convinced there would be a demand for such a thing. In fact, we weren't even sure we'd buy one. And if we wouldn't, then why would anyone else?

The Electric Bath: great in theory...

Know your audience

Richard's boss at the time, a glamorous account planner that he fancied called Cathy, had recently pointed out that the most important thing to do when setting up a business was to understand your target audience. Richard at that point did pretty much whatever Cathy said, so this piece of advice was taken very much to heart. And it reminded us that the only audience the three of us could credibly claim to understand was ourselves and our friends. So we next tried to think of something that would make our own lives a little bit easier and a little bit better.

At this stage we were 26 and living and working in London. There may be better places to be a twenty-something with no real responsibilities, but there aren't many. It's a great city, and there's always something going on. Which basically means it is bad for your health. We were working long hours, followed by late nights, with no time for exercise and a diet skewed towards beer and pizza, with fruit and veg only making an appearance on rare trips home to our parents. We realised there were a lot of people in the same position as us – who wanted to be healthy, but found that there was just something about modern urban life that conspired against it.

So that was the problem we wanted to solve: to make it easy for people to do themselves some good. And to make it taste nice too. From identifying that 'need' we thought of ways to solve it, and pretty soon we got to smoothies. Delicious, natural fruit crushed up and put into bottles so you could grab one on the way into work. A habit that, for once, would be healthy.

It was a simple idea that we understood – it was about getting fruit into bottles and then into people. It was a physical product that we knew how to make at home (which we naively thought meant it wouldn't be too hard to work out how to make lots of them). But most importantly it was something we ourselves wanted to buy.

'So how do we get it into bottles?'

Better, not different

We recognised that although we'd come up with an idea that solved a real need, it still needed to do so better than anyone else's. At first, this can feel a bit daunting. But most good ideas don't need to be world-changing revolutionary new inventions. The UK is full of eccentric inventor-types, locked in their garden sheds working on their secret designs, emerging seven years later with a huge beard and a new gizmo, most of which are too weird and wonderful to have any commercial future. And while there are some notable exceptions in this area – Trevor Baylis and his wind-up radio, James Dyson and his cyclone technology – most successful business comes from improving on something that already exists, rather than inventing something new, entirely from scratch.

We certainly didn't see ourselves as inventors. And while some people have credited us with 'inventing' the smoothie (or at least being the first people to bring them to the UK), we didn't. A brand called Pete & Johnny (aka PJs) was already selling bottled smoothies in the UK. This was a good thing, in that it meant a market definitely existed for smoothies, but a challenge in that we had to find a way to make ours a better alternative to theirs.

To do so, our approach was simple: we'd make ours the natural way. This was in contrast to PJs, who made their smoothies from concentrates, a gloopy syrup made from low-quality fruit juice. Yes, using concentrates made things more profitable and easier for them as a manufacturer, but it meant the taste and nutrition was compromised.

In other words, the consumer[1] lost out. Instead, ours would be made from all-natural pure and fresh fruit, with nothing added or taken away.

[1] We don't like the term 'consumer'. It's commonly used to denote a great big mass of people who will behave predictably, which is a load of nonsense, seeing as people behave in all sorts of odd ways for no reason whatsoever. So we prefer 'drinker', which is OK but can sometimes feel a bit twee. Of course, we should be able to use 'consumer'. Consumers = people who consume. But it has patronising undertones, so when we use it, please rest assured that it's hurting us more than it hurts you, as you can tell by the length of this overly long footnote.

Ideas we've been pitched

Over the years, people have pitched their business ideas to us. Sometimes it's good to get a second opinion. What's more, we understand the plight of the entrepreneur and should be more able to see the potential in their smart business plans. But sometimes the idea can be a little 'niche' in its appeal. Here are the three weirdest ideas we've been pitched.

The Cat Bag

We all know the problem – your pristine sofa has cat hairs all over it because Pumpkin likes to snuggle up to you while you're watching The One Show. But have no fear, for the Cat Bag is here. It's an all-in-one plastic boiler suit for your cat that prevents its hair from getting everywhere. Of course, this idea does present a few problems, at least in our eyes, mainly centring around the area of animal cruelty and cat toilet habits. But who knows? We might have got it wrong.

Baby Blender Bottles

Getting fruit into your baby's diet can be tricky. But not any more. The Baby Blender Bottle looks a bit like a regular baby's feeding bottle, except it's got a small blender mechanism in the bottom. So you can chuck in some fruit and whizz it into an instant smoothie. However, we weren't that keen on the proximity of baby's face and hands to the spinning metal blades, so we turned this one down.

Dog Nappies

Pretty self-explanatory. Dog nappies. Nappies for dogs. In one fell swoop they would rid our streets of doggy doo doo, and our parks would be clean and clear again, with no need for dog owners to do that inside-out thing with a plastic bag. However, there's something just not right about seeing a dog in a nappy. Like a giraffe in a balaclava. And would you really want to change a dog's nappy? Thought not.

The granny test

Like most good business ideas, ours was clear and simple. The world of commerce rewards simplicity and its associates, clarity and focus. So it's always worth applying the granny test – can you explain your business idea and how it will beat the competition in a simple sentence that your granny would understand? In Hollywood they use the same principle when movie execs sell film ideas to studio bosses – they call it the 'elevator pitch' – 30 seconds to explain the concept. The theory behind the Granny Test is that if you need three paragraphs to explain your idea and strategy, it's probably too complicated or unclear to take root in the business world. We use the Granny Test on any new product we're about to launch – we ask: what's the simple clear reason people would buy it over the competition? We've learnt over time that the products we've launched that have failed have been the ones where we couldn't explain their purpose and benefit over what else was out there.

Keep the main thing the main thing

So granny has done her bit, and you have a simple insight about what your product or service is going to do better than anyone else's. Now the trick is to put all your time and energy behind delivering that difference. We call it keeping the main thing the main thing. Every decision you make needs to somehow get you closer to achieving that point of difference. We gained hugely from having this clarity. Our main thing was keeping things natural (it still is). That meant we knew what to say when people suggested using flavourings or preservatives. It meant we could brief the people we were working with on what was most important to us. And it meant that even after nine months of trying to get the business up and running, with a succession of confusing meetings, we at least had the benefit of never losing sight of what was actually important and what we were trying to achieve: make a proper, natural smoothie, with none of the nonsense that other people got up to in the food industry.

If she gets it, they'll get it

To this day, a lot of the success we have had with innocent stems from getting our big idea right. Spotting a real need, born of our own experiences; developing a product that directly solved the problem and that we would buy; having a simple, clear insight about how to make ours superior; and keeping focused on delivering that main thing.

The patented, no-nonsense, having-an-idea-to-start-your-own-business checklist (just in case you couldn't be bothered to read the last few pages)

1. Follow the need
Have a look at the world around you. Where's the gap between what people want and what's available? Which day-to-day problems need solving?

2. Know your audience (it could be you)
Understand your target audience, which will be easier if it's you or your peers.

3. Think better, not different
You don't have to reinvent the wheel. Just make a better one.

4. Remember the granny test
If you can't explain it to granny, don't do it.

5. Keep the main thing the main thing
Identify your main thing and stick to it. Make every decision based on whether it gets you closer to your goal.

chapter two
start small, but do start

Start small, but do start

We've been pitched enough concepts over the past few years to know that most people have an idea for a business inside them. However, the majority don't even begin working on the opportunity, mainly because the whole project seems so intimidating. Basically, it's hard to see how you're going to build yourself a global multi-billion-dollar business when you're sat in your kitchen nibbling on a biscuit.

But the cliché is true: every business in the world started small. M&S began life as a market stall, and YouTube was started recently by two friends in a room above a pizza takeaway; it's now worth over £1 billion. Even in today's heavily competitive world, little can still get big.

Our advice is simple: start small, but do get started. There's nothing like taking the first small step to help get you over the initial fear and inertia that surrounds creating your own venture. Once you've committed to action, you'll find momentum comes from the pitter-patter of those first baby steps.

We started small. We sold our first smoothies in the August of 1998 from a market stall at a music festival we used to organise in Parsons Green, London (see box opposite). Selling smoothies from a stall wasn't our big idea. Our dream was to have a proper company, selling drinks through shops all over the country, but we didn't know how to get to that; it all seemed so unreachable. And while we had done a lot of research and recipe development in our evenings and weekends, we didn't have the confidence to give up our jobs and tackle the project full time.

That lack of confidence came from not knowing whether people would like the smoothies enough to part with their hard-earned cash to buy them. We had tested them on our friends and family but they weren't what you would call an objective audience (if your own mum doesn't like your product then you know you're in trouble).

Jazz On The Green

After leaving university we still kept on trying our luck in the world of music. We lived near a patch of open space called Parsons Green in West London and used to organise a small music festival there every August. The idea was to bring the community together to enjoy some music and hang out in the sun. The event was called Jazz on the Green (jazz was the only type of music we could get a licence for, but we used to slip a few other things in there on the day). The event was free, and raised money for charity. It was a popular weekend with those who came along, but pretty unpopular with some of the local residents.

In the first year, we completely underestimated the number of portaloos we needed and 5000 people turned up. Nature took its course. Following the event the Hammersmith and Fulham Gazette ran the frontpage headline, 'Rivers of urine flood Parsons Green.' We'd just like to apologise to the local residents (again), and especiallly to the local vicar; his churchyard did not do well.

So we decided to take a small first step, and make smoothies to sell at the forthcoming festival to see what people thought.

At this point, we lived in a shared house in nearby Barons Court (where we had been testing our smoothie recipes in our kitchen), but now we needed a way to get a thousand or so bottles for the music festival. Through a bit of luck and by asking around we met a farmer called Jeff who was deeply, and we mean deeply, in love with carrots. Nearly 80 years old, he had grown carrots all his life and even had his own tiny carrot juice pressing plant at the edge of his carrot fields.

Jeff loved carrots and carrot juice so much he would get up in the morning, go out into his fields, pull up some carrots, drive them to his factory as fast as his tractor would take him and squeeze them into delicious fresh juice. Then he would drive the bottles down to London in his car and sell them to the handful of shops that stocked his drinks. The thing he was most proud of was that he could get his carrots from being in the ground in his fields in Nottinghamshire to being juice in a bottle on a shelf in London in less than six hours. It was a completely ridiculous business model, and we loved it. And him.

He may have been more than 50 years older than us but we shared the same humour, and belief that food should be kept natural, simple and fresh. He also had an attitude of 'there's nowt we can't do if we put our minds to it', and he agreed to make a batch of smoothies for our test market. So we invested £500 in buying a load of fruit and ended up with our first 1000 bottles of smoothie to sell at the festival.

At this point, we didn't have a name, or any packaging. To get help, Richard approached Rich and Andy, a creative team in the ad agency he worked at, known for coming up with smart, original ideas. They came up with the name 'Fast Tractor', so called because of the speed the farmers (inspired by Jeff) would drive their tractors at to maintain the freshness of the fruit.

It was certainly different, if not somewhat cryptic, but we'll always take weird over average. The team also had a friend who would design the label, so we decided to give it a go. The result was nothing if not distinctive (see below).

The same creative team cracked another problem for us. We needed to know what people thought of our trial smoothies at the festival. To do so, we had designed a detailed two-page questionnaire for people to fill in – age, gender, how much they liked the taste, how much they liked the label, etc etc. But as much as we wanted to know the answers to such questions, we couldn't help but think it was a bit much to ask people to fill out a complicated form when they were at a music festival with their friends.

Fast Tractor – a tremendous brand name and look for a high-performance diesel product...

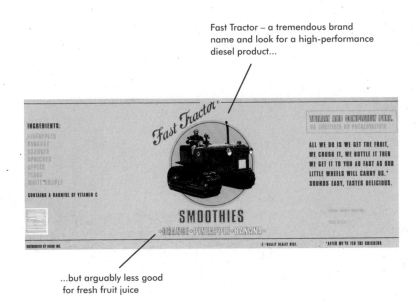

...but arguably less good for fresh fruit juice

HOW FARMER JEFF MADE HIS CARROT JUICE.

START

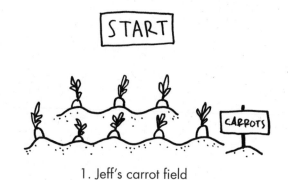

1. Jeff's carrot field

2. Jeff's Fast Tractor™

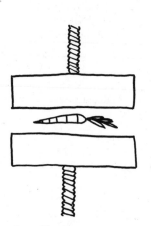

3. Jeff's carrot press

4. Straight to London

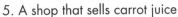

le Café

5. A shop that sells carrot juice

STOP

From field to fridge in six hours.

Rich and Andy listened to the problem and said, 'Don't you just want to know if people like them or not?' to which we nodded our heads. Their suggestion was to keep it simple. Put up a big sign above the stall that asked, 'Should we give up our jobs to make these smoothies?' and place a bin in front of the stall that had YES written on it and a bin that said NO. Then get people to vote with their empty bottles, by chucking them in the appropriate bin.

So that's what we did. Jon manned the stand over the weekend, while Adam and Richard ran the event. The stand was nothing more than some bales of hay, some big buckets filled with ice to keep the drinks cold and the aforementioned sign asking people to tell us what they thought using the latest in bin voting technology.

At the end of the weekend, we had sold out of smoothies, and the YES bin was full. There were a few bottles in the NO bin (probably from our mums trying to persuade us from giving up the decent jobs we had at the time). Either way, it meant that the decision was made. We were going to make smoothies for a living. The Bins Test (as it is now known) was our first major milestone; it had cost us next to nothing, but gave us that crucial impetus to quit our jobs and commit to the next stage of setting up the business. It was that all-important first step; we had got started.

Heads we go back to work...

We've told the Yes and No bin story lots of times over the years.
And while it is entirely true, it is not quite the full story...

When we got together after Jazz on the Green on the Sunday
evening, although the Yes bin was full, we were still nervous
about giving up our jobs and contined to um and aah about
taking the plunge. So we agreed to toss a coin to make the
decision for us. We each called tails and tossed the same coin
three times. It came up tails three times in a row. We took that
as a sign (to stop dithering) and resolved to resign the next day,
which we duly did.

We subsequently kept the coin and it became known as The
Chairman. It was blu-tacked to the office wall and in the first few
years when we couldn't make a decision between the three of us
we would call on The Chairman to decide.

Small is cheap

Ten years on, we continue to 'start small' with any new initiative we embark upon, be it establishing ourselves in a new country, launching a new product or testing out a new marketing campaign. It allows us to be more entrepreneurial – we can test ideas quickly and without breaking the bank. And if a new product, country or campaign shows potential, we then put serious money behind it to accelerate the growth and make the most of the opportunity. Basically, we beg and borrow to get a test away cheaply, and then invest in the ideas that work.

We applied this 'start small' approach when testing whether innocent would work outside of the UK. Our mission is to get healthy drinks and food out to as many people as possible, so international expansion was part of the plan from early on. However, the idea of selling in Europe still made us apprehensive. We had no idea of how to set up a business in a foreign country. None of us had any experience of doing so and we spoke very few languages. But rather than ignore the opportunity or spend months doing academic market research, we decided to test the idea by starting small and giving it a go. So our first 'international business' was one person, in one country, selling to a few shops in one city: Dublin.

We chose Dublin for simple reasons: no language problems, pretty close to home and most importantly because we had found an excellent person – Matt Henchie, aka The Henchdog. Henchie initially sold our drinks into a few delis and cafés by walking in off the street with a big smile and some free samples. By signing up a few stockists and getting a decent rate of sale, it proved that innocent could work there. Matt found a wingman called Pete Oden and they worked from Pete's house in his shed. As the business became more established, and as Pete and Matt got us stocked in more places, we then invested more in the Irish business. Over time, they moved out of Pete's house into Dub Towers, which is still the home of our bigger Irish team today, and Ireland has grown to be our second largest market.

We did the same to test innocent in France. One man, one van, and a lot of hard work to get some trial listings to see if the brand would work. As you would expect, mistakes get made by doing things in this 'quick and dirty' way. Perhaps the most embarrassing was launching with the proud claim of 'pas des préservatifs', which we thought meant 'no preservatives', but in France translated as 'condom-free'. Not the message we intended, although it was at least true. But we got stocked in a few outlets and delivered a good rate of sale, and it proved that innocent could sell in France, which gave us the confidence to apply more resources to build on those foundations.

It's a model that works well for us – start small, prove something works, then invest behind it (we talk more about accelerating growth, and coping with it, in chapter 4).

Pete in our first Dublin office, aka his shed,
complete with AstroTurf

From small acorns

One of our favourite things at innocent that originally started small is our Big Knit campaign, where we put little woolly hats on our bottles to raise money for charity. This was the brainchild of a man called New Adam (when he joined we already had an Adam, so he was christened New Adam). He came up with the idea of putting hats on our bottles and for each one sold we would donate 50p to Age Concern to help keep older people warm during the winter months (20,000 older people die each winter in the UK because they can't keep warm, and New Adam wanted to do something about that). New Adam's pitch involved getting volunteers to knit the hats by hand. We thought he was nuts. Who would knit them? Where? How will they get onto the bottles? There was no way it would work.

In this case, there was nothing better than being proved wrong. In the first year New Adam got over 3000 hats knitted by grannies up and down the country. By year two this increased to 20,000, then 80,000, and in 2008, with Sainsbury's helping out and asking their staff and customers to help knit, over 500,000 little woolly hats were knitted, by people from the age of 7 to 97, from our mums to Paul Smith, raising over £250,000 for Age Concern. A beautiful example of what you can achieve if you're prepared to start small.

New Adam – woolly thinker

The Big Knit: how it happened

We found some friendly ladies who taught us how to knit properly

Jon, Richard and Adam got involved. To varying degrees of success

Our drinkers sent in their hats by the sack load. Literally

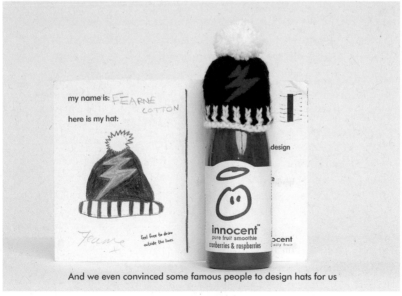

my name is: FEARNE COTTON
here is my hat:

...design

feel free to draw outside the lines

innocent™
pure fruit smoothie
cranberries & raspberries

And we even convinced some famous people to design hats for us

Of course, starting small doesn't mean you can't think big. Why shouldn't you set yourself the goal of becoming the next Starbucks/Oxfam/Celine Dion?[2] As long as you get started, there's no end to what you can do.

One person we really admire who proves that point is Jeremy Gill. A few years ago, he was a struggling actor with a career that wasn't going too well. He decided to rethink his life plan, and woke up one morning and realised, like all self-respecting actors, that he should contribute to world peace. So far, so Oscars. But Jeremy's approach was different: he had a single, simple goal. What about just one day of peace? A campaign to get an internationally recognised, 24-hour ceasefire period – where all armies put down their guns, and allow charities and medical workers to enter war-torn areas and deliver much-needed supplies and aid.

Jeremy launched his Peace One Day charity. From his parents' dining room. With no money. And no experience. Four years later, Jeremy found himself in the United Nations in New York watching 191 member countries approve Resolution 219, a decree that officially recognised 21 September as an international day of peace, backed by everyone from Nelson Mandela to Angelina Jolie to Kofi Annan. All this from persistently pursuing an ambitious idea that started small in his bedroom.

In short, the main difference between those people who are successful and those who aren't, is that the successful people are the ones who actually got going. You can have the greatest idea in the world, but it remains just that if you do nothing about it. Obviously, once you've got your idea, there is a tremendous amount of work to cover to make it a reality, but when it comes down to it, the most important thing you can do to make your business successful is to just start.

[2] Although maybe one Celine is enough.

The Eastenders Test

Want to know whether you've got the drive and determination needed to set up a successful business?

Set yourself the challenge of writing a business plan for your idea in the evenings when you get home from work. If you don't have the drive to do this while you're still doing your day job, you probably won't have the resilience and drive to set up and run a successful business. As tough as it is to put in a full day at work and then come home to face more spreadsheets and timing plans, it's a great test of your resolve.

And if you're putting it off each night and watching When Pets Turn Bad instead, it may be a sign that you haven't got an idea that excites you enough, or maybe you're not committed enough yet to go through the pain of setting up a business.

chapter three
keep on keepin' on

Keep on keepin' on

While taking the first small step is fundamental, when setting up a business there will be many more steps still to take. The ongoing process is time-consuming, frustrating and confusing. You start out knowing absolutely nothing, and it can take a long time before things start to fall into place. You will also be told your idea won't work by a lot of different people.

But don't lose heart, it will be worth it. Keep asking questions; try different solutions; and above all else, don't ever, ever give in. Whatever problems you face, there will always be a way.

Little white lies

We soon learnt that things weren't going to be as easy as we had originally and naively thought. Having taken the first small step with our YES/NO bins test, and the rather larger one of leaving our jobs, we were now faced with the challenge of translating our small-scale experiments to the mass market. How could we make our smoothies on a large scale?

Adam called his friends at Virgin Cola, and questioned them on how to make drinks commercially. The advice was to work with a 'flavour house', a company that helps develop drinks and source the ingredients. It sounded promising. Adam called one recommended by his ex-boss. After the call, Adam couldn't be clear, but he thought the flavour house may have inadvertently got the impression that he still worked for Virgin, not that Adam was calling in his personal capacity as a director of a company with no name and no product. The fact that Adam cadged a favour and we held the first meeting at Virgin Cola's head office probably didn't help clarify matters either.

It was a slightly awkward situation – Trevor, the man from the flavour house, probably thought he was about to land a big fish, whereas the three people sat in front of him were plankton. We didn't dare ask whether he thought it was for Virgin, in case he lost interest.

We desperately needed someone to work with, but an embarrassing conversation was clearly looming on the horizon. 'I tell you what,' said Adam, as the three of us discussed the issue following the meeting, 'let's clear things up later, once the work has been done.'

We moved forward with the flavour house, and spent days in their kitchens working with their fruit and our recipes to make up drinks, testing them out on friends and family to see which ones people liked best.

In tandem with this we discovered another area we had absolutely no experience in – selling directly to shops. Could you just walk in straight off the street into a store and try to sell food products? Did you need a certificate to prove your food was safe? Were you allowed to simply start selling or did you need a licence? Basically, we had no idea.

We decided the best way to find out was to just do it. Adam got his friend at a design agency to create some simple labels for a smoothie brand that we called 'Fresh n Fruity', we made up some strawberry and banana smoothies, filled up ten bottles each and stuck the labels on with Sellotape. Hey presto, the imaginatively named 'Fresh n Fruity' smoothie was born.

We split up, each with a cool bag, and visited ten stores, assuming we would be chased straight back outside. But most store managers were happy to chat, would try the drinks, and six out of ten wanted to order some. That was the only time the whole exercise got slightly surreal, because we then had to explain the company wasn't real and the smoothies weren't available, resulting in the managers quite rightly asking why we were in their stores trying to sell drinks that didn't exist.

But that afternoon taught us what we needed to know: that there were shops out there prepared to purchase smoothies from us, even if the labels were Sellotaped on. And we also learnt a lesson that we've held dear ever since: the best way of testing something is to do it. Don't get lost in academic research – make it, test it, see what happens.

Back in the world of the flavour houses, our NPD (new product development) was not going well. Their recipes used concentrated orange juice, but we wanted to use freshly squeezed as that was how we did it at home. So we decided to part company. And we never did quite clear up the Virgin thing. Sorry, Mr Branson. Sorry, Trevor.

So started a long, drawn-out process to find a way to produce our drinks the way we wanted them to be made. At first, we thought we might need to set up our own smoothie factory, but we soon realised that wasn't the right answer (see next chapter). It became clear that we needed to find a manufacturer to work with. We spoke to pretty much every drinks company in the UK. They all said the same thing: that our idea wouldn't work. The general consensus was that if you wanted to make smoothies you should use concentrates to make them more profitable, flavourings to enhance the taste lost in the concentration process, and preservatives so they wouldn't go off. We said we just wanted to use fruit, like you do at home. They patiently explained that we didn't understand, the juicing industry didn't work like that. We patiently explained that *they* didn't understand, and that this was our business idea – if we didn't keep things natural, we didn't have a business.

Everyone, however, was incredibly helpful. We would ring the head office of a big drinks manufacturer and ask to speak to the MD and be amazed to find ourselves talking to her or him a few moments later, arranging a time to come in and see them. We would always ask for such meetings to start at 1pm since we were completely broke and the possibility of free sandwiches was a big deal for us.

A real low point was when we found ourselves driving down the M4 to a meeting with one of our last remaining leads. Our company vehicle was Adam's Fiat Uno, a second-hand car he'd had since he was 17. It had over 160,000 miles on the clock, and a single electric window that Adam had fitted himself as a teenager, which was now broken and permanently stuck open. It was pouring with rain as we drove down the motorway and we got soaked. As we got out of the battered car in our ill-fitting and now dripping-wet suits, the people

After the rain came the fire. As the car was being driven through Willesden Junction in the year 2000, en route to delivering an innocent branded fridge to a health spa in Watford (the Uno had now become the company's lead delivery vehicle), the engine caught fire. Dan jumped out quickly and the fire brigade were called to douse the flames. The Uno was no more.

we were going to meet were watching us from their office window.

It was the first and hopefully last time we'll ever leave a wet patch in a company's reception area. They took us into a room, handed out hot drinks, fed us lots of sandwiches and sent someone off to fetch towels. Having seen the state we were in, they even offered to pay for our petrol for the drive home, which was a genuinely touching gesture.

Again, they unfortunately couldn't help us. They didn't handle fresh fruit, only the regular flavourings and concentrates of the soft drinks industry. But they did give us a lucky break. They knew of a man from Jamaica who had moved to Wales and had started a business importing fresh oranges, and who now made fresh orange juice. Maybe we should talk to him.

We have to confess, when we chatted to Jamaican Mike on the phone, and heard his broad Jamaican patois proclaiming 'Yeh mon, ting sounds alreet', about our idea, we assumed those words were not coming from the mouth of a small, slightly rotund white guy. But Mike was a bit of a rarity. We can't say for sure how many Welshmen there are who have been raised in Jamaica and then returned to Cardiff to set up a fresh juice business, but we only needed one, and we'd found him.

As Mike already handled fresh oranges to make his juice, he figured he could make our recipes too. He wasn't convinced it would work – blending smoothies from 100% fruit would be expensive, but he said we had the same spark in our eyes that he had when setting up his company and so he would give it a go. So after a few trials, we committed the money for the extra kit necessary to make our drinks in his place, and finally, after 12 months of searching, we had found our supplier.

It honestly will take longer than you think

If you're setting up a business, whatever length of time you think it is going to take, triple it, and then add some more. Everything takes longer than you think. We gave ourselves one month, and it took us nine. As a result, we financially ruined ourselves.

If possible, continue in an existing job for as long as you can. Not only do you retain a source of income, but assuming you don't take the mickey too much, a workplace can provide resources, contacts, opportunities for market research and, most importantly, free sandwiches and coffee. It may mean working yourself to the bone, but there are many business ventures that never got off the ground purely because the founders could no longer support themselves.

That long, drawn-out search to find a manufacturing partner taught us a key lesson. Put simply, success is about resilience. When others are telling you something can't be done, keep going until you prove them wrong. Find the yes, when everyone is saying no.

How the entrepreneur's brain works

Do you know anyone rich?

Something that was even harder than finding a manufacturer was searching for an investor. We had no experience, no product and no name, although 'Massive Risk' would have been appropriate. But the one thing we had was a robust business plan. It saved us from complete failure initially, and at the very least got us some meetings. The colour-coded charts were a thing of beauty, along with some pristine spreadsheets, all set on the finest paper on offer (from the office stationery cupboard). It contained the research on our basic proposition, our target market and costs versus retail prices. Most importantly, it showed a path to profitable growth and the rationale for investing.

We started our search for funds by going to the bank. A good idea, we thought. Banks have money. (Or at least they used to, back in the good old 1990s.)

We were encouraged by an initiative called the Small Business Loan Guarantee Scheme, where the government underwrites loans made by banks to start-up businesses, thereby de-risking the loan for the bank, and making it easier for new enterprises to get access to cash. Although not in our case. After we were turned down by the twentieth bank in a row, we took the hint: government guarantee or not, no bank was lending us their money.

But without the cash, we couldn't start our business at any significant scale, so we continued looking. This search took us to the world of Venture Capital firms – companies whose very raison d'être is to invest money in start-up businesses in return for shares.

There are a lot of such companies in London; there are thick directories full of them. We got such a directory, and tried all the VC companies that were in it. They were nothing if not consistent. The answer was no, and the stated reason was clear – the business would not work. To quote one VC at the time, 'You score zero out of five in the investor's handbook – you're too young, you're all friends, you've never run a business before, you've no experience of the sector and you'll be competing against the world's biggest food and drinks companies. It is a dreadful investment opportunity.'

He decided not to invest.

Although not forthcoming with the money, the VC community were helpful and said we should try to find a private investor, an experienced individual who would take the risk and put in the start-up capital. And some of the VC companies suggested people to talk to. We chased every lead, but after many presentations, false starts and subsequent rejections, we simply ran out of options. This was nine months into having left our jobs. By this point we were financially exposed, with big overdrafts, reliant on friends for drinks on nights out. Reduced to eating breakfast cereal three times a day, at least we all managed to drop a dress size.

But then we got a break. An organisation called London Business Angels Network hosted a quarterly session where start-ups looking for funding could come and pitch to their members, *Dragons' Den* style. As a group, they made over 100 investments a year. They were exactly the people we needed. And we had managed to bag half an hour at their next meeting.

And that's how we found ourselves stood in front of fifty potential investors, having given the pitch of our lives, requesting that if anyone was interested in finding out more, could they put their hand up.

And not a single person did.

That hurt.

It's quite hard to not take it personally when you have been rejected by your government, every bank in the country, every VC firm in London and by the very community of people that actively say they want to invest in start-up businesses.

At this stage, we contemplated throwing in the towel. Without an investor we couldn't start the business, and no one wanted to invest.

Disheartened, we explained the problem to a friend, who mentioned the rule of 'six degrees of Kevin Bacon' – that everyone on the planet was in theory only six people away from knowing Kevin. Beyond this being good news if you were a fan of *Footloose*, the theory might just mean that we would know someone who knew someone who was rich enough to invest. In fact, he argued, if we asked enough people we may even be able to get Kevin Bacon to put money into our company.

And that's how Kevin Bacon came to invest in our smoothie business.

Actually, that last bit isn't true. But the 'Kevin Bacon principle' meant we tried a more random approach and sent out a cheeky email that simply said '*Does anyone know anyone rich?*' in the subject line. We posted that email to every address we had, and lots we didn't. Essentially, we spammed London. We got two responses, one from a previous boss of Richard's who happened to be having a passionate affair with a wealthy tax exile in Monaco (he chose not to invest but we enjoyed the juicy bit of gossip) and the other from an old work colleague of Jon, who had done some work experience in the office of a man who occasionally made investments, a Mr Maurice Pinto.

So we sent Maurice our business plan. And unlikely as it was, after nine months of being told no, of pitching to every company and bank we could find, after virtually resigning ourselves to pulling the plug, we met Maurice and following a rigorous testing process, he said yes. Just on the point of giving up, we tried a different route, and we got the money.

We learnt something that day. Success is not determined by age or intelligence or race or gender. It is not determined by divine intervention or by the school you went to. It is determined by whether you are determined; whether you keep going or not. And by whether you ignore the people who say it won't work and prove them wrong.

A reconstruction of the time we
sort of met Kevin Bacon

Richard Branson sums it up in his most oft given piece of advice: **never, ever give in**. And this applies whatever stage you're at. Whether you're starting up or established and growing. No matter how bad it feels, it is never over. There is always a way, there is always another option. You just have to find it.

As an aside, our Richard's dad once told us a story from his childhood when he was at the same school as Paul McCartney. On the last day of term, everyone brought in their favourite toy. The young McCartney brought in his guitar, and was sat on a wall strumming it. His English teacher, who apparently didn't like Paul very much, came up to him and sneeringly said, 'You'll never get anywhere playing that, McCartney.' Ahem.

Maurice's gamble

When we went to see Maurice, the man who became our investor, he agreed to put in £50,000 out of the £250,000 we needed and promised that he would get the rest of the money from the five other individuals he did deals with. They were a group of friends and Maurice was the lead investor; in 20 years of doing deals together, when Maurice put his money in, they did too.

But for the first time ever, they turned him down flat. This put him in a tough spot – he committed to us that he would get the money but his co-investors thought it was a bad deal. So he had to either let us down or stump up the cash. He decided to honour his original commitment.

Four years ago, he told this story at a talk he was giving. A person in the audience asked whether he put the extra money in out of obligation or because he thought it was a good investment. He said he had done it more out of obligation and he thought he was going to lose the money, which shows what a principled man he is.

Still, he now loves winding up his investor friends, saying innocent has been his best ever investment and reminding them that they said it wouldn't work.

never, ever give in

(find the way that works)

cut this out and stick it on the fridge

chapter four
coping with growth

Coping with growth

In our experience, having a strong, simple idea, starting small, and being persistent are the three most important things when going through the hard yards of setting up a business. But to become and remain successful, you need to have a business that can cope with growth, and you need a strategy that is going to deliver that growth in the first place. In other words, in addition to the hard work and determination, you have to make the right commercial and strategic decisions: Should you manufacture yourself or have someone else do it on your behalf? What opportunities should you pursue, and in what order? And have you got the funds to do it all?

Whether we knew it at the time or not, there have been some decisions we've made at innocent that have been fundamental to the success of the company. If we'd got these decisions wrong then the way innocent has been able to grow would have been materially affected. So we thought it may be useful to talk them through to help frame some decisions you may be facing with your business.

Outsource or DIY?

When we settled on the idea of setting up a smoothie business, one of the earliest decisions we faced was whether to build our own juice factory or work with someone else's. At first, we assumed we would have to build our own factory, not least because no one else was making products like ours, and if we worked with another company, what would stop them stealing our recipes and selling them to other people?

But we soon realized that teaming up with a manufacturing partner would be a smarter move, for a wide variety of reasons. Firstly, building our own plant to squeeze and bottle would require millions of pounds, and would mean from the outset we would have the overhead (and headache) of running a factory. Secondly, it didn't play to our strengths; running a manufacturing site takes a lot of specific skills and experience, none of which we had. Thirdly, it meant that we could focus on growing the business and building the brand rather than worrying about managing a factory. Fourthly, it has allowed us over time to be responsive to what our consumers want. For example, when we started doing one-litre smoothies our drinkers said they would prefer for them to be in a carton not a bottle. If we had been running our own manufacturing site, we would have had to either invest in a new carton-packing machine (which would have cost literally millions of pounds) or continue to use a plastic bottle that our drinkers didn't ideally want. But because we outsource the packing, we could go to a manufacturer that already had a carton line and put our fruit down it.

Partnering with manufacturers has enabled us to fulfil our rapid increase in sales without the need for large amounts of capital. If we had built our own squeezing and bottling sites, innocent would not be the size of business it is today.

Fruits are sourced by us through our direct relationships with growers and processors.

The fruits come to Europe's fruit port in Rotterdam and are blended in a chilled blending site.

Then they're taken by sea and road to our UK bottling sites where locally sourced ingredients are blended.

The packed smoothies are taken to a central chilled warehouse and then sent quickly on to the stores.

Which is where you pop them in your trolley and take them home.

Conversely, there have been some parts of the process we have deliberately *not* outsourced. Most importantly, we develop the recipes and source the fruit ourselves. At the end of our day, smoothies are nothing but fruit, so whoever finds the best fruit and creates the tastiest recipes will most likely have the best product.

To this end, we have invested over the years in our Get Closer to the Fruit and Product Development teams – the agronomists, sustainability experts, fruit buyers and recipe developers that find the highest quality, most sustainably grown fruit and turn it into the best-tasting recipes.

With each season, our collective knowledge of the world of fruit grows exponentially and becomes ever more valuable. As this expertise is retained in-house, it means we can guarantee our smoothies remain unique to us and are made from the world's best fruit, but bottled in a factory that we don't have to own. In other words, we have invested in developing the most value-adding part of the process in-house, and have outsourced the most capital intensive stage. It's a combination that works well for us.

When it comes to your business, it is always worth thinking through where the real difference is created and where your key strengths lie, versus the parts of the process that are relatively commoditised, which other businesses can do better. Own the value-creating areas, and let partner companies focus on which of the other bits they do best. That way, everyone wins.

Peel, chop, blend, taste. All in a day's work for an innocent recipe inventor

Get Closer To The Fruit

Our Fruit Team will do anything to find better ingredients, even if it means drinking homemade booze with Serbian farmers (bottom left).

WHEN WE GROW UP
WE WANT TO BE
INNOCENT
SMOOTHIES

Do less, better

Several years into the business, we realised that our 'start small and try lots of things' approach was almost running away from us. Our small tests in Ireland and France had evolved into permanent businesses, and momentum was gathering to launch in other countries too. But at the same time, we had been developing and testing a range of new product ideas (frozen smoothie desserts and natural cereal bars among other things), and we were thinking about launching them properly.

These additional projects were putting a lot of strain on everyone, especially as we were already under pressure coping with the growth in UK smoothies. Remembering our own advice of 'keep the main thing the main thing', we realised we should focus on either countries or categories, rather than try to do both simultaneously.

We debated which opportunity to go after first, and soon chose getting our smoothies to new countries. The logic was that smoothies were a brilliant product to establish everything that innocent stood for – healthy, natural, tasty food and drink. And when innocent was known in these new countries we could launch other products later.

Once we had decided to focus on new countries over new categories, we had to choose between the US and Europe. Again we looked at the pros and cons of each. The pros of the US were that it was a big market of over 350 million people, with only one currency and one language, and there were retailers who were actively asking to list the product. In Europe, to get to the same number of people, we would have to trade in many different countries, each with their own language, laws and, in some cases, currencies. But the issue with America was that we would have to start up a whole new supply chain; our fresh products would never make it from here to there. In Europe, however, our test markets showed we could serve the Continent from our manufacturing base in the UK, and there were 15 different countries within a 24-hour drive. So the answer became clear – Europe represented a much better ratio of effort to reward than the US.

Of course, deciding to go after Europe was one thing, then we needed the strategy for how best to capitalise on the opportunity. Should we do it all ourselves as we did in our test markets, franchise out the brand or set up joint ventures with other businesses?

The short answer is that we have tried it different ways in different markets, and through trial and error the strategy has become increasingly clear. We now know if the market size is relatively small, such as Belgium or Finland, it's best to find a distributor to partner with who will take responsibility for selling our smoothies into their retailers; this means we don't incur the cost of having to set up a business in the country, but can still have our smoothies sold there. On the other hand, where the market is potentially big, such as France or Germany, we want an innocent team on the ground to make the most of the opportunity. Certainly, all things being equal, having a team in the country is our preferred route.

When we commit to building a team in a new market, we typically first find a leader from that country using our network and headhunters; ideally it will be someone with experience of running a business, and it certainly has to be someone with the entrepreneurial drive needed to set up innocent from scratch in that region. We then help them recruit a small team, consisting of people both from Fruit Towers in London and from the country in question. That blend of innocent and local know-how is a great combination, with both sides bringing useful experience.

But irrespective of whether we have an innocent team on the ground or whether we work with a distributor, the strategy for getting the brand up and running is the same. We typically start in one city or region, normally the capital of the country. The first job is to get stocked in the beacon outlets (the best food and drink places in the city), to get seen in the right places and get some sales coming in. Then we use PR, sampling and simple things like having our grassy vans out on the road, to get the brand on people's radar. As more people get to hear about the company, we push hard to get stocked in more places, including ideally signing up a high-end supermarket chain that will give us some volume. Once a decent density of distribution has been achieved in a certain region, we then invest in a regional advertising campaign to drive up sales. If this is successful, we extend the sales coverage nationally and follow up with a national advertising campaign.

This makes it sound easier than it is, and it's taken plenty of expensive mistakes to get to this level of clarity. But overall, moving into Europe has been one of the best decisions we've made. It is a dynamic and fast-moving market. And in our first three years of being on the continent our sales there have increased from €2 million to €6 million to €16 million, which is nice.

A map of the countries where we sell our drinks. We're working on the rest.

Make sure you have access to cash

A final critical thing is to make sure you have access to the cash to grow once you've got successful foundations in place. Fundamentally, growth is expensive. The sales may not come as quickly as you hoped, there will be hidden costs you didn't realise, and you will inevitably make mistakes and end up sinking money into things that don't work. All of this is normal and to be expected. But it means you need to have the money to make the most of each situation. There is nothing worse than seeing an opportunity melt away because you don't have the cash to go after it.

For us, Europe is a classic example of this. Continental Europe represents a huge upside for innocent; we've got our smoothies to market in 13 different countries, consumers love the product and the brand, our sales have been growing fast and the market is increasing rapidly. But we are now up against big businesses in each market, who both outspend us and can get distribution quicker. It became clear to us that if we wanted to make the most of the European opportunity, we had to increase the pace of our expansion and for that we needed additional investment.

As a result, we kicked off a fund-raising process in September 2008 (just when the world financial market went into meltdown; nice timing). We hit the headlines when we secured the funds, as our new minority investor was Coca Cola, and some people thought this was us 'selling out' and going against everything we stood for.

Interestingly, the opposite was true. All of the money raised (Coke invested £30 million in the company in return for less than 20 per cent of the equity) was paid into the business (not to the shareholders) to fund our growth in Europe. innocent remains a stand-alone company, with Adam, Jon and Richard continuing to lead the business, and Coke have no decision-making powers over the way the business operates. Also, importantly, the cash came with Coke's offer to help us get our healthy drinks out to more people – be it through introducing us to customers, assisting with distribution in

Europe or simply being there to ask for advice from time to time. It's a great opportunity to help us do more of what we're here to do.

The fund-raising process we went through also taught us several things, the most important being: *be careful of the conditions people attached to investments*. We had several offers of cash from investors other than Coke, but when we got into the negotiations they came with some pretty scary small print. One potential investor offered to put in the money, but we would have to stop donating money to charity. Another potential investor said they would invest the cash but they would want control of the business. Both conditions were against our basic principles. On the other hand, Coke's offer came with no such conditions; just a desire to help us achieve our financial, social and environmental goals, with us in the driving seat. So for us it was clearly the best way forward. And meant we got to carry on with our mission of getting more healthy products out to more people.

'You've sold your soul to the Devil'

Most people, the majority of our drinkers included, thought the Coke deal was a smart move. But a small vocal minority were upset with us. We knew some people would have a strong reaction to the news, so we were completely transparent about the deal, and put it on the front page of our website, on our blog and in the newsletter to the innocent family.

About 300 people complained. A lot of the people that were originally upset were happier when they realised innocent was staying a stand-alone business, being run by the same people in the same way, and that we had done our due diligence on Coca Cola and found them to be a company full of decent, ordinary people. But there were definitely some others who remained against the deal for their own reasons, and they did not change their view. While we obviously felt differently to them, we will always respect those with an alternative point of view to us, and we let everyone have their say – you can see the debate on our innocent blog.

One thing's for sure, everything we have been about – making natural healthy food and drink and getting it to as many people as possible; pushing hard for more sustainable ingredients and packaging; and supporting charities in the countries where the fruit comes from – remains intact. And with the funds coming into the business, we get to do more of these things than we would have done otherwise.

chapter five
know what you
care about

Know what you care about

If you're ever going to read a proper business book, may we recommend one called *Good to Great* by Jim Collins? In it, Mr Collins and a team of business school graduates research and identify the main differences between businesses that are merely good and those that are great. Trust us; it's more interesting than it sounds.

One of the main differences they identify is that successful organisations – social, commercial or otherwise – have a very clear sense of purpose. Or, to get existential for a moment, they have asked themselves (and answered) the biggest question of them all: why are we here? In other words, high performing organisations, and everyone within them, understand the reason why they exist and what they're here to do.

What's my motivation here?

Answering the Why question, and having everyone in your team buying into the answer, brings a myriad of benefits, each with a commercial edge. Firstly it helps to engage and motivate people. Knowing you're doing something worthwhile encourages people to come into work every day rather than stay at home and watch *This Morning*.

You may not have heard of howies. They're a company based in Wales that make clothes for people who skateboard, ride bikes and do outdoor stuff. Their claim to fame is that they're Cardigan Bay's third largest clothing company (in case you're not familiar with Welsh geography, Cardigan is a small town in west Wales with a population of 4200). If you're ever passing through, why not pay them a visit? David and Claire, the couple who set up the company, make a lovely cup of tea, using a proper teapot and everything.

But even if you just check out their website, you'll be struck by something. You'll get a sense that howies is a company with a vibrant, deeply felt sense of purpose. It runs through everything they say, and, most importantly, do. Ingrained in howies is a desire to show that

JIM COLLINS

GOOD TO GREAT

Why some companies make the leap... and others don't

GOOD TO
GREAT

JIM COLLINS

RANDOM
HOUSE
BUSINESS
BOOKS

there is another, better, more responsible way of doing business. This purpose shows itself most convincingly in the choices howies make – the fact that they produce clothes only from natural fabrics and recycled materials, that they levy an Earth Tax on themselves to raise money for environmental causes, and that they use their marketing to drive awareness of social and environmental issues. You don't do all that just to sell more T-shirts. You do it because you believe it is important, and because you want to. And the team at howies are motivated because they know they are doing something more than just selling T-shirts (which are great by the way. The one below is our favourite).

Knowing your purpose also helps guide the choices you make as an organisation. General Electric, one of the world's most successful companies, has a clear purpose – 'To turn imaginative ideas into products that help solve the world's toughest problems'. That purpose helped GE several years ago identify the commercial opportunity to develop technology that tackles climate change. And following years of multi-billion-dollar investments in their green industries, they are now one of the world's largest wind turbine and solar panel manufacturers.

A sense of purpose also acts as a beacon, transmitting a signal about what you're here to do, not just to guide those people already in the organisation, but also to attract like-minded people who could come and help. Ultimately, done well and sincerely, it's a kind of self-selecting recruitment tool. On the front page of their website, Amnesty International state their purpose as being 'to protect individuals wherever justice, fairness, freedom and truth are denied'. For a lot of socially aware people that's a compelling call to send in their CV.

Right from the beginning of innocent, we were at least clear about one thing: we wanted to make it easy for people to do themselves some good – to get natural, healthy drinks out to as many people as possible. We didn't talk about it being 'our purpose' because we hadn't read the management books at that point, but there was a motivation beyond the financial for setting up the company: we wanted a business that helped improve the diets, and therefore health, of our consumers. It was something we could be proud of.

Seven years in, we revisited our purpose, to check it all still rang true. We also wanted to hear the views of all the people who had subsequently joined innocent and were helping make innocent possible – what for them was the ultimate purpose of the company? It was a worthwhile exercise, and involved asking every single person to contribute their thoughts, mainly in groups over lunch with cheese sandwiches.

Reassuringly, the spirit of our original 'purpose' remained; we just simplified and refined it. We agreed our overall purpose was to **'Make food good'**, a purpose that covers our three biggest beliefs when it comes to food and drink:

1. We should make food that tastes delicious and re-engages people with how wonderful natural, non-messed-around-with food can be.

2. The food we produce should be genuinely healthy, made only from ingredients that are positively good for you; which, without putting too fine a point on it, will help people to live a bit longer.

3. And the way we make it should be sustainable. To push for ingredients grown and made in a way that is environmentally and socially responsible, and has a light ecological footprint, so it is better for the people involved in making it as well as for those people eating it.

Staying true to our purpose will give us the best shot at achieving our 30-year vision of innocent becoming *'the Earth's favourite little healthy drinks and food company'*, our goal of building an international, healthy, earth-friendly brand that makes delicious, nourishing, natural drinks and food, universally available for all. It is a mission we feel strongly about.

Having a purpose: some pointers

A purpose should not be primarily financial. It is too generic and will not guide and motivate long term. If you truly only want to make money, you might want to consider a career as a crack dealer. We hear the profit margins are just fantastic.

This is not to say that making money does not matter. It does; it's crucial. But it is not the purpose.

This may sound a bit heavy, but a purpose should appeal to the moral instincts of your team members, and be founded upon people's deeply held ideas about what is right and worthwhile.

The purpose also has to be relevant and specific enough to give direction to a team and its individuals to guide them in their day-to-day actions. 'Make the world a better place' is probably going to be a bit too vague.

When agreeing a purpose, get the input of everyone you work with. Everyone's views are important. That said, the purpose must resonate most with the person running the show. If they're not buying it, why would anyone else?

Accept that some people may not share your chosen purpose, or think you are plain nuts. But be transparent about what it is, so that people can then decide to either commit to it or move on.

Make sure that everyone does one of those two things. (You don't want passengers. Or worse, snipers.)

Most importantly, purposes that rhyme are best. Annoyingly for us the word 'food' doesn't rhyme with the word 'good', even though it looks like it should. On balance we decided to accept this, rather than go with 'Make food gude'.

we make healthy

If there's one thing we care about, above all else, it's making food that is genuinely good for you, naturally.

Each bottle contains at least 2 portions of fruit, a gentle nudge towards your 5-a-day

With 5 different types of fruit in every bottle, you get a wide spectrum of different nutrients

Because we use whole crushed fruit and not just the juice, you get the fibre, the flesh and all of the other good stuff

Our smoothies are low-medium G.I. meaning that their goodness and natural energy is released slooooowly

innocent
original fruit smoothie
cranberries & raspberries

smoothies

Our veg pots contain 3 portions of veg. Have one with a smoothie and that's your 5-a-day sorted. Your mum will be proud

At under 300 calories and low in salt, they're the healthiest thing you can buy in a pot

Each one contains nearly 100% of your GDA of fibre so you'll feel nice and full

I'm new

innocent
tasty veg pot
Moroccan squash tagine
with giant cous cous
& fresh coriander

1 pot = 3 portions of veg

veg pots

(Right, sales pitch over, now back to the book)

Get some values

Businesses, in one respect, are like hotel rooms: they can corrupt. There's just something about the pursuit of profit that can tempt people to do things they normally wouldn't do.

Obviously, successful businesses need to grow revenue, save costs and make money. We're as keen to do that at innocent as any good company. We chase growth and profit because it creates opportunities and value. But if within your business hitting the numbers is the *only* requirement, weird stuff is going to happen.

Enron is business history's most compelling example. It ultimately imploded because the *only* thing that mattered to Enron was the numbers. In Enron's world it became acceptable to deliberately short the supply of power to California so the Enron trader could sell electricity at inflated rates, because doing so was immensely profitable. And it was OK to post potential profits from future businesses as real profits in your current year's budget, as it made that year's performance look great. The company became so obsessed with reporting great numbers, it not only stopped caring whether its activities were legal, but actually stopped caring whether they even existed. That seems pretty stupid.

But it happened. Enron is the logical extreme of what can go wrong if a business chases profit with no guidance on corporate behaviour. That's where values come in – they provide a simple set of guidelines and rules to play by; a few non-negotiable principles that govern your behaviour, shape the culture and capture the DNA of the business.

To put it another way, decent values prevent businesses, in their pursuit of profit, from behaving like idiots.

We've got five values. (Five is our magic number – see our Rule of Five in a few pages.) We use our values all the time. We use them as a filter when recruiting people (if people don't personally resonate with the values of innocent, they're not going to get the best out of innocent and we won't get the best out of them, so we don't employ them). No new starters get through their induction period without Richard spending an hour with them banging on about the values. We develop people in line with our values, and we reward people for living them. We ask people to leave if they act against the spirit of them. In short, we take them seriously.

Our innocent values

Natural

The most important value. This applies first and foremost to the products we make – they must be 100% natural, 100% of the time. But the thought of keeping things natural goes further than that – we want people to be their natural selves at work; to bring their own personality to the business, and to use their own personal values when making business decisions. We want people to be conscious of the fact that the business is a community of human beings, and therefore the more we treat each other in a natural, friendly manner, the better it will be for us all. The golden rule is to treat everyone we come across, especially our drinkers, the way we would want to be treated – honestly, openly, warmly, naturally.

Entrepreneurial

It's the most difficult one to spell, but it's in our blood. We're an independent company, set up from scratch, and we want always to act entrepreneurially, chasing opportunities, challenging the status quo and finding the yes inside the no. We want people to take risks, and to try new approaches. This is not to say we condone stupid, reckless decisions; we want and expect people to think things through, but we will always back the person who has tried something and failed over the person who never tried anything new in the first place.

responsible
entrepreneurial
generous
commercial
natural

Our values – we like them so much we hung them
next to our baby photos

Responsible

We know it makes us sound a bit like a Miss World contestant, but we want to leave things a little better than we find them. This works on every level – from the smallest scale, such as not leaving your tea bag in the sink, to taking responsibility for the social and environmental consequences of our business actions. This value is at the heart of why we invest in environmentally conscious packaging, why we measure and reduce our carbon emissions each year, and why we pay a premium for ethically grown fruit. We also adhere to the spirit of 'don't be lame'; a catch-all reminder to help people avoid acting in a slightly rubbish way. It basically means don't lie, don't let people down, and don't 'forget' to replace the toilet roll if you finish the last one.

Commercial

This one's here so that we don't sound too much like a bunch of hippies. We don't want people to think we're something we're not. innocent is a business, not a commune (although some of us wear a white gown to work on Fridays), and we are about growth and profit and the opportunities those things bring. We encourage people to be commercial – to negotiate in a tough but fair manner – and we employ people who can keep focused on the main thing and nail whatever needs doing. Basically, we need those rare people who are socially aware and commercially astute in equal measure. For us, one does not negate the other. In fact, we know we can't meet our long-term social aims for the business without looking after the commercial side, and the opposite is equally true.

Generous

Being generous is our final value and it applies everywhere. Generous with feedback, always starting positively, telling people what was good so they can do more of it, but also letting people know what wasn't good enough and what they could have done better. We also want people to be generous with the time and help they give to each other, whether that's lending a hand unloading the van or helping the person you sit next to think through a problem. The company needs to be generous too, firstly to the people who contribute to making innocent successful. Our profit share, anniversary options, nest egg and bonus structure are all part of implementing our philosophy in this area, namely that everyone should get something, and the people who contribute the most should receive the most.

And finally the company needs to be generous to the communities it impacts and is dependent upon. That's why from the day we started we have always given a minimum of 10% of profits to charity each year.

How we wrote the values

At first we thought it was a bit too corporate to have a written set of values. We reckoned people would get what we meant by 'being innocent', just by osmosis. That works when you're small and everyone is in the same room and can hear all that's going on. But as you get bigger, people become less exposed to each bit of the business, and don't get to pick up on everything. So it makes sense to get what is important codified. It's an obvious point, but it makes it easier for people to follow common themes if they know what they are.

When we decided to sort the values out, there were 41 people in the company, and we made sure everyone was asked to contribute their ideas. It was simply a question of asking people what we cared about, what we were for and what we were against. One version had us down as being against guns and pro cheese. Certainly true, but not so relevant on a day-to-day basis.

Doing it this way meant we got a better, truer sense of our values. It wasn't one person dictating them from above, but a representation of the collective conscience of the company. If your business is trying to come up with its values, we really would recommend spending the time hearing what everyone thinks they should be. Mainly because everyone's going to have to live them. Seems only fair.

Just in case you were wondering...

We have a rule of...

Whenever we write a strategy, a series of objectives, a set of tasks for the day or even just a shopping list, we always remember the highly scientific Rule of Five. The theory goes something like this:

1. *Everyone can remember one thing.*

2. *If they can't, they're a doofus.*

3. *Most people can remember three things.*

4. *And no one can remember more than five.*

5. *That's the Rule of Five.*

chapter six
it's all about the people

It's all about the people

It's a universal truth about business that irrespective of what your company does, you're going to spend most of your time dealing with people – their hopes, issues, talents and pay demands. That's either a scary thought or an exciting one, depending on your disposition. But if you're leaning towards the former, you may want to rethink setting up a business or taking on that new leadership position.

Everything in the end comes down to people; a business is ultimately nothing more than a community of human beings. Whatever a business does or doesn't do is a direct result of someone in that work community doing or not doing something; of caring or not caring; of being capable of the task, or not. So if you want your company to be successful, focus on the people. And look after them; after all, they're the ones looking after your business.

Find your dream start-up team

Starting a company from scratch requires a wide variety of skills – developing products on the one hand and writing P&Ls on the other; talking turkey with the bank manager and selling turkey to the shopkeeper; impressing investors with your strategic insights and then unloading the vans. Setting up and running a business is multifaceted so we are in awe of people who do it by themselves.

Our advice: get a small team together of people who share the same values but bring a different and complementary set of skills. And start from there. If you get the right people in place first, the rest will follow.

We didn't find it difficult to decide on our start-up team: the three of us were it. After having the idea on the snowboarding trip, we held our first meeting the following Saturday at Jon's company's offices in London. It felt a bit naughty coming in to use their posh client meeting rooms without their permission, but it felt pretty good too, especially when we found where the biscuits were kept.

Our first task was to determine who was going to do what. It took five minutes. We each knew what we were good at, and what we were bad at, so we assigned responsibilities accordingly. Richard – marketing. Jon – operations. Adam – selling (and eating the biscuits). At the time, we didn't realise it, but we had the ideal dynamic for an effective start-up team – a group of people who have different but complementary skills, who share a set of values and a common goal, with clear areas of individual responsibilities. In a decent start-up team you don't want people who are all good at the same stuff – you'll miss crucial areas, tread on each other's toes and duplicate work. Aim for a small group of people, aligned around a common goal and each doing what they do best.

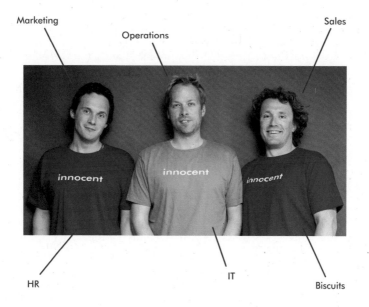

Marketing

Operations

Sales

HR

IT

Biscuits

On working with friends

We started the business as friends. And ten years in we're closer than ever. It is not uncommon for us each to work a 50-hour week, say goodbye to each other at 6pm Friday as we leave the office, and then find ourselves round the same table having dinner at 8pm, this time with partners and other friends too. People ask us what it's like working with such close friends. And the short answer is, brilliant. You can trust each other implicitly. You know each other's strengths and weaknesses. You can speak bluntly. Plus it makes the whole process more fun.

From the beginning we had some unwritten rules about working together. Don't talk shop outside work hours. At work, hold each other to account and make sure that professional standards are adhered to. And keep communicating – the most important of them all. We meet every Monday at 4pm for an hour to make sure we are all on the same page with whatever's going on that week. And we meet once a quarter off-site to make sure that we are still aligned longer term. These away-days are valuable, focused sessions, although they do have a tendency to occur on Friday afternoons, which then leaves the evenings for us to engage in less work-related activities.

Weirdly, the only arguments we've had have been about interior decoration. On the big stuff – which country we should launch in, what product is next etc – we talk things through until we're aligned or we defer to the expert whose area it is. But we've had blazing rows in the past about the colour of the office wall, the colour of the office floor, and our biggest ever argument, which was all about the placement of some bookshelves.

Getting people on the bus

In any evolving business, there will be the need for more people. And if there is one thing to take seriously, it's recruitment. A business can only ever be as good as the people that work in it. So sweat the details over who you ask to join your company and 'get on the bus'. It's the most important business decision you ever make.

Don't take our word for it; we've learnt it from one of the world's greatest companies: Google. They set up in the same year we did, and while we've grown to over 250 people, they have grown to over 12,000 in the same time period. It's a stunning achievement and makes us eat humble pie every time we think about it. But the most surprising thing of all is that one of the two founders still signs off on every person they employ. Larry and Sergey see the decision of who they ask to join Google as being the most important business decision they ever make.

We stole their idea. We figured if Larry at Google can find the time to personally sign off each employee in his 12,000-strong workforce, we can do the same with a team of 250. It slows down the hiring process a little, but we've found that when it comes to recruitment, if you act in haste you repent at leisure.

Know what you're looking for

In order to get great people to join your business, you first have to know what you're looking for, otherwise you're essentially handing your recruitment over to the dual forces of chance and pushy head-hunters, which is not a good mix.

When we first started recruiting, our selection criteria was something we called the Van Test. The basic principle was: did you think you could spend three hours in a van with the person, and find it enjoyable? It was a good mental check to ensure they were people we were excited about working with.

As things grew, we recognised the need to be more robust in identifying what we were looking for in people. Over time, we've identified the three essential things – Values, Capabilities and Experience, in that order.

1. Values – These days we've got a codified set of values (natural, entrepreneurial, responsible, commercial, generous – see chapter five) that are less van-based, and we look for people who personally chime with them. Testing this is largely instinctive, although people's CVs, and in particular their extracurricular activities and outside interests, give clues about their underlying nature. We like people who are proactive, who have a track record of improving things and adding to the communities in which they belong. It could be that they set up a mini-business when they were a teenager, or ran a charity project or led a team in a social, work or sporting capacity. We want people who do things that show passion and commitment and original thinking. In short, we want entrepreneurial, generous people who make life a brighter and more interesting place.

2. Capabilities – If we think they match innocent's values, then we want to check that the person has got the capabilities to do well in the business. We set practical challenges to test they have the right skills to make a success of the role they're about to do. If it is a commercial role, can they sell and negotiate? If it is a financial role, can they read and run a P&L? And are they smart generally? Anyone who joins us will have to, at some point, do a job they've never done before, so we need to test whether they have the latent capabilities to tackle new problems, to learn as they go along. We test for this ability to think around problems with our annoying interview questions. Contrary to how it may feel if you're on the receiving end of such a question, we don't ask them to catch people out, simply to check how they think (see overleaf for an example).

3. Experience – While having the values and capabilities are mandatories for getting a role at innocent, having the experience, while always desirable, is not something we necessarily insist on.

After all, the business was founded by three people who had no experience of running a business or making smoothies, so we know that energy, commitment and smarts can sometimes compensate for not knowing what you're doing.

Our position on this changes with more senior people, however, where we've learnt experience is critical. With senior people you're paying for someone who has been through a comparable situation before, so they can avoid the pitfalls a beginner may fall into. And you need them to lead in the right direction from the beginning – taking a large group of people down the wrong path can get messy and expensive very quickly. So, the more senior the role, the more we look for relevant proven experience.

Our favourite interview question

A classic question we ask to check people's latent intellectual skills is 'the cinema question'. It splits into two halves.

The first part is: taking your local cinema as an example, estimate roughly how much revenue it will make in an average week.

We give people a pen and a piece of paper and ask them to walk us through their thinking. People usually go blank for a second or two, and then their synapses fire up. Most manage to break the problem down into its constituent parts – the number of seats in a screen, the number of screens in a cinema, the number of performances per day and the typical attendance at each. Good people spot that different times of the week will have different attendance levels, and that there are two tiers of ticket prices to take into account. Great people also think about revenues from food and drink sales and make assumptions about that, and include advertising as a third source of cash.

This part of the question simultaneously tests problem-solving, logic, mental arithmetic and commercial awareness.

The second half of the question is: imagine you are given the cinema to look after for one Saturday and you have to drive the profits as hard as you can on that day alone; what would you do?

This is to test their commercial awareness of how money is made and to see if they can think creatively in a commercial setting. A good answer involves people coming up with some low-cost, practical ways to drive people into the cinema, and, most importantly, to sell them more stuff when they are there. Have people understood the concept of margins, and that popcorn and drinks are massively profitable so you need to sell as much of these as possible? What other things can they think of selling that will be low cost and high profit? We push people hard on this; after all, we need entrepreneurial, creative, commercially aware people.

So it is a tough question, but it puts everyone on a level playing field – it transcends people's age, CV, qualifications and background; it gets down into the detail of how they actually think, of how smart and savvy they are. And these are good things to know if you're thinking of doing business with them.

Finding what you're looking for

So getting clear on what you're looking for is an essential first step. But finding people that meet the requirements is a constant struggle; it's the bane of every successful business in the world. You need a 24-hour-a-day approach to attracting a great team. You need to always be communicating what you're looking for to potential employees, and you need to constantly pick up on any interest talented people may be showing.

We do various things to bring this 24-hour 'always promoting, always looking' mentality alive:

1. **Talk up the business** – we're not shy when it comes to this. On our website, when we're out at a trade show, via the press, at our neighbour's dinner party: we're always promoting the values of the business and what it is like as a place to work. If we don't tell people what we're all about, then no one will. We want to attract the people who are attracted to what innocent stands for.

2. **Job ads on the labels** – we have millions of bottles on shop shelves every week. Each bottle has a label with a space for a message on it, and every so often we use it to mention job vacancies. We've found some great people through doing this.

3. **Internal headhunting fee** – if an innocent person recommends someone for a job, and that person gets the job, then a substantial fee will be paid – anything from £2000 to £5000. We trust personal recommendations.

Keeping people on the bus

Once they're on board, the focus shifts to making sure you keep the great people. Like most things, we don't get this right all of the time, but over the years we've become increasingly clear on some of the most important things to do to keep good people engaged for longer. These are our top seven things:

1. Be clear on what you want

When it comes to engaging people, we've found the single most important piece to get right is ensuring people are clear on what is expected of them. To this end, every January, each individual works with their manager to agree five objectives for the year – projects they are going to complete, results they will deliver. We spend a lot of time on this, and ensure there is a line of sight between the individual's objectives and those of the company. This clarity on what each person should be doing, and how it contributes to the bigger picture, helps build motivation: high-performing people want to be clear on what success looks like so they can focus on delivering it.

2. Tell it how it is

The more feedback people get, the better they perform. We are strong advocates of real-time feedback – it is baked into our values. If people are told (on the day) when they've done something good, and what was good about it, then they are more likely to do it again. And likewise if you let people know on the day when something wasn't up to scratch and how it could have been better, they can change it. There is nothing worse for an individual to not be told that things weren't good enough. If they don't know that, they're not in a position to improve.

3. Measure performance

Having objectives is important so people know what to do. Measuring performance against those objectives is equally important to make sure people know how they're doing. Twice a year everyone at innocent has their performance measured, primarily against the objectives they've signed up to deliver. We all get a score from one to five, where five is an absolute star and constantly exceeding expectations, and one is repeatedly falling short of your objectives and it could be time to move on. It sounds a bit harsh, but the clarity means everyone knows where they stand and it is a thousand times better than being polite and never saying what needs to be said.

We'd rather have a hole...

For the first few years in innocent we had a 100% retention rate, and were very proud of it. But we came to realise that while a strong retention rate is a good thing, 100% was too much. A healthy business will always see some people move on. Either there will be some individuals struggling to meet the demands of their job or they'll have skills different from those required in their role. In situations like this, it's essential that the individual is told transparently about what needs to improve. And they should be given the opportunity and support to close the gap. If they can't get there, then it's in everyone's best interests for them to move on.

We think the only time people shouldn't get a second chance is if they are polluting the values of the business. A temporary shortfall in performance can be rectified; a deliberate attack on the core values is more serious.

One of the most memorable things we've ever heard in business was a line uttered by Dan Walker, former Head of Talent at Apple, who was talking at a conference on talent management and made the point that if businesses wanted to remain strong they had to get rid of 'snipers' – people who prided themselves on being anti the business. A polite English woman in the audience asked what to do if you had no one to replace the person. He looked her right in the eye and replied with the immortal words, 'Well, honey, I'd always rather have a hole than an asshole.'

4. Provide opportunities to learn

Development and change are good. The opposite is stagnation, and stagnant people smell like ponds, so we like to have people continually raise their game. Of course, the person who has to lead this is the individual themselves. In reality, if the person isn't committed to developing themselves, their boss won't be – no one cares more about a person's career than the person themselves. The role of innocent is to provide opportunities to learn and a culture that supports and encourages people to lead and challenge themselves.

We provide learning opportunities in various ways. One area is through our in-house training programmes. We run a programme of residential training courses known collectively as the innocent academy. Each lasts two days and covers different topics – the art of presenting, how to negotiate, problem solving, the principles of finance, etc. All the modules are written and taught by people at innocent. This in itself is a form of training – there is no better way of learning something than having to teach it to others. It is a way of learning that we learnt from the principle of medical school – where doctors acquire their practical skills through an approach of 'watch one, do one, teach one'. It also means the knowledge stays within the collective brain of the company, and it's cheaper too.

We also have a training budget per person for that individual to invest in 'craft' skills relevant to their career choice, be that formal qualifications in accountancy or gaining access to the latest thinking in product development. And furthermore we have a study grant that people can apply for to fund longer term studying to improve their skills – part-time MBAs, marketing diplomas, etc. We'll support people who are serious about improving their skills.

There are small things too – we pay for any business book that a person buys and reads as long as they donate it to the innocent library afterwards. And some of the brightest people in innocent have set up their own learning networks – groups of contemporaries from non-competing, inspirational businesses, who share knowledge and best practice. It's possible that you might come across people from

Pret A Manger, Google, What If, Apple and Lush Cosmetics, sitting together here at Fruit Towers to discuss their respective approaches to finding and looking after great people.

Of course, people will ultimately learn the most by doing the job, so we make movement within the company as fluid as possible. If people commit and do well in their current role, the business will flex itself to create opportunities that will stretch them in a new role. Which explains why we have people who started as receptionists who end up organising music festivals, finance people moving to marketing and operations specialists moving to the commercial team. As we have got more established we have formalised this approach with twice-yearly talent planning sessions where we make sure the stars in the business get to move round and take on new roles.

5. Share the proceeds

If people are working hard and doing good things, they need to be rewarded for it, otherwise the implicit deal breaks. Our approach to remuneration is that 'everyone should get something, and the people who contribute the most should get the most'. This is made tangible in several ways. Firstly, we have a Profit Related Pay scheme. If we beat our profit target, we pay out a proportion of the profits to the team. Secondly, everyone gets some options in the company after they have completed their first year. It's not a lot and it won't change anyone's life, but it means everyone will get something if the business is sold one day. Then we have a scheme called The Nest Egg. This gives people the opportunity to buy shares in the company at a heavily discounted rate. And depending on their performance rating, we also match, double or triple what they buy. Finally, pay is reviewed once a year, and rises and bonuses are again related to the performance rating of the individual. Basically, everything is tipped towards making a career at innocent mutually rewarding for the people that really contribute to the business. Therefore remuneration is not distributed evenly, but it is distributed fairly – in line with what people deliver.

6. Keep communicating

It's unrealistic to expect people to care about things they don't know about. And we want people to care about the business, so we invest a fair amount of time in keeping up to date with how it's going. We use all means possible to share information. Every Monday morning at 9am the whole business gets together for 30 minutes, and each team gets one minute to say what's happening in their part of the business. It's a good way to start the week, and a great opportunity to get a bit sweaty by doing some group exercise, which we do in a quasi-religious style at the end of each meeting. (It's as cringeworthy as it sounds, but does get everyone smiling on a Monday morning – no mean feat.)

We also have a brief monthly company update, where we review the performance of the business, so people are kept up to date with how the business is doing. And once a quarter we have a bigger company meeting to review the longer term strategy and performance of the business. Everyone's invited, everyone contributes, everyone learns something they didn't know before.

Finally, a company wiki, sitting at the heart of our custom-built intranet, acts as a fluid and democratic place in which to spread news and dump all of the knowledge we accrue. (It's also a source of good gossip about who's hot for who at the moment.)

We also consult people before bigger decisions are made. By doing so, not only are people more engaged, but the company benefits from having more brains thinking through the issues of the day. For example, we did this at the time when we were debating whether we should sell our smoothies in McDonald's. We got everyone together over lunch and asked people what they thought. Different views were expressed, burgers were eaten, and we used what we'd heard to help make our decision, which was to pitch to have our kids' smoothies sold in their restaurants. Asking people what they think leads to better decisions.

Our Monday Morning Meeting
– mic check

7. Do the soft stuff

All of the above things are the priorities, the important mechanisms to get right first. But we're fans of doing the smaller, softer stuff too, to help make innocent a better place to spend 40 hours a week. Everything from providing as much free breakfast as you can eat/drink (a healthy breakfast gets a person's brain working, so go figure), to the innocent scholarship, which awards people £1000 to go off and do something that they really want to do (cycle across Uganda, become a UEFA qualified goalkeeping coach, train as a zookeeper, visit India to learn the sacred art of chutney making – it's *Jim'll Fix It* for grown-ups). There are big nights out after company meetings, free yoga on a Wednesday (taught by Richard's glamorous wife) and co-funding for a wide variety of clubs, from wakeboarding to life drawing to the most popular of all – the innocent cheese club.

Free private healthcare hopefully gives people one less thing to worry about if they are ill, and subsidised massages and free smoothies help people not get ill in the first place. We have our Lord and Lady of the Sash award, where once a month people vote for the person who has added the most to life and work at Fruit Towers. And in good years, we have an annual event called the Nature Weekend where the whole company decamps from Fruit Towers for an adventure abroad. As with all the best ideas we've had, this one came from following a need, in this case the founders' need to go on a skiing holiday.

We know these things are the froth 'n' frills – the chocolate flake in the workplace ice cream cone, if you like. And they should never take the place of the important things – the training and remuneration devices, the clear objectives and real-time feedback, and all that other good stuff. If all you're doing is the frothy stuff to keep people motivated and happy, it won't work. It'll feel empty.

Focus on the important stuff. Share the big ambitions throughout the business, get people figuring out how they can do their bit to make it happen, and be completely transparent with everyone about their role and performance. If people know why they're on the bus and how they're doing, they'll enjoy the ride a whole lot more.

Class of 2000 (minus the lady in black)

Class of 2001

Class of 2003

Class of 2004

Class of 2005

Class of 2006

Class of 2007

Class of 2008

chapter seven
now that's what we call marketing

Now that's what we call marketing

If you're setting up or running a successful business, you're
going to need a marketing strategy. The trouble is, people have
different definitions of what constitutes such a thing. To some, it is
simply having a name and a logo, proudly displayed at the top
of their company stationery. To others, it's the adverts and jingles
commissioned by the marketing department, designed to delight
people during the ad break. To us, it is nothing less than our entire
business, defined as much by the way we drive our vans and answer
our phones as it is the products we sell and the way we conduct
ourselves with our customers. Because in this interconnected,
marketing-savvy world, **everything you do, say or are, communicates.**
So when it comes to marketing your brand, everything is important
(although some things are more important than others).

What's your promise?

Great brands stand for something. They promise something relevant
to their potential consumers. Like the would-be president in election
year who campaigns under a banner of 'Hope' or 'Experience' or, in
a brand's case, 'Smarter trousers'. All professionally managed brands
are clear on what their promise is. And up and down the land, in the
hallowed halls of the most revered biscuit manufacturers, you will find
that most sacred of all documents – the brand strategy template, upon
which the brand's promise will be dutifully transcribed, often in the
blood of the junior brand manager.

So if you want a marketing strategy to establish or sex-up a brand,
start by working out your brand promise. It should be derived from
a combination of what your brand cares about and can deliver,
and takes account of what your target consumers actually want and
what the competition are not offering. As such, it should be simple,
motivating, distinctive and true.

And then, make sure your product or service delivers against it. There is no more important part to your marketing strategy than the product or service actually fulfilling the brand's promise. At innocent, our promise is to make stuff that tastes good and does you good, naturally. And we deviate from this at our peril. It is fairly safe to say that we will never sell a range of Cheezee-Choco-Doughball-Bitez™. To break our promise like this would divest our brand of its credibility and, worst of all, make it appear untrustworthy. A bit like finding the 'Family Values' politician in bed with a goat.

But while ensuring your product or service delivers its promise is the main thing, it is not the only thing. You will still have to bring that product or service alive – to get it noticed, desired, talked about and remembered. And for that, you need to use the dark arts of marketing, which if you're not careful can get very expensive, but if done right can sometimes be harnessed for free.

The dark arts of marketing – a low-cost guide

When we were trying to raise funds to set up our business, we were given many reasons why the business wouldn't work. The most common one was that we couldn't compete against the big boys and their huge marketing spends. Potential investors explained how the juice category in the UK is dominated by Pepsico (they own the Tropicana and Copella brands) and how their multi-million-pound advertising budgets would obliterate us.

The job of the entrepreneur is to prove people wrong, but we had to admit they did have a point. Our marketing budget was essentially zero, which not only meant no long lunches at the Ivy with the advertising agency, but also left us nervous about how we would get our brand noticed.

However, if necessity is the mother of invention then a tight budget is the father of doing stuff on the cheap. And because we had to communicate, but didn't have the money, we found ways of doing so for free. We found the following things to be the most important.

1. Choose the right stage name

With no money for advertising, choosing the right brand name is important; the name itself must communicate the brand promise and what you stand for. It also needs to be memorable and distinctive, so it sticks with people like a good stage name. And to us it was also important to have something we'd be happy to see on a T-shirt, as we'd be wearing them most of the time. But we couldn't think of a moniker that met all these requirements.

It wasn't like we hadn't tried. Since the days of Fast Tractor and the YES and NO bins, we had come up with hundreds of names. But none that quite worked. We liked Naked, but it had already been taken. We considered Angel smoothies for a while, but went off it. A friend had suggested Hungry Aphid. Someone pitched in with the name Monkey Vomit, but we couldn't see that one making it big in Sainsbury's.

Ultimately we got to the name 'innocent' in a dull and geeky way. It came from looking in the thesaurus in the reference library in Huddersfield, Richard's home town. Starting with the words 'natural', 'healthy' and 'pure', he looked up other words that related to them. And again with the words that came from that search. We built a long list of contenders and scored each against our criteria.

We found the original document of the different names recently, so we put it in here, overleaf. It's really embarrassing for us to read the criteria we were judging the names by, especially 'intangible cool factor'. Weirdly, 'Seedy' came first, which is a terrible name. innocent scored well, but was marked down a point for being 'a bit aromatherapy'.

But we slept on it for a couple of days, and everything it suggested – pure, natural, unadulterated – was what we were all about. Plus, it was more memorable than your average juice company name, and thankfully it passed the T-shirt test.

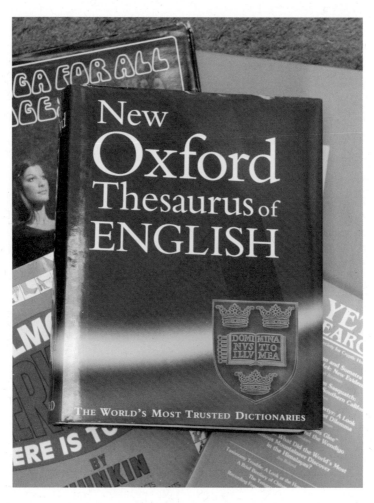

Our saviour – the book that delivered us from
the clutches of Monkey Vomit

possible company names as assessed in January 1999

New Open Save Print Import | Copy Paste Format | Undo Redo | AutoSum Sort A–Z Sort Z–A

Sheets Charts

	A	B	C	D	E	F	
1		**CRITERIA**	Communicates the nature of the drink	Does so in a non-corporate/slightly kooky way	Pr-able	Is not too fashionable	Cou club
2		**NAMES**					
3		Naked	2	2	2	2	
4		Exposed	2	2	2	2	
5		Newborn	2	2	0	2	
6		Stripp'd	2	2	2	2	
7		Nude	2	2	2	2	
8		Native	2	2	2	2	
9		Primitive	2	2	2	2	
10		Wild	2	2	2	2	
11		Innocent	2	2	2	2	
12		Simple	2	1	1	1	
13		Naïve	1	2	1	2	
14		Sinless	2	0	2	2	
15		Easy	2	2	0	1	
16		Paradise	2	0	0	2	
17		Uncut	2	2	1	0	
18		Raw	2	1	1	1	
19		Single	2	1	1	2	
20		Direct	?	1	2	2	
21		Glorious	2	2	1	1	
22		Splendid	2	2	1	1	
23		Nostrum	1	2	1	1	
24		Babylon	2	2	1	1	
25		Seedy	2	2	2	2	
26		Bambino	1	2	1	2	
27		Love Apple	1	2	1	1	
28		Hula Hula	1	2	2	2	
29		Freshman	2	2	1	2	
30							
31	**KEY**		**COMMENTS**				
32	2 = Good		I think there has to be something in the straight-to-you thought				
33	1 = OK		Maybe, also something in the Island/Juices from Jamaica thought				
34	0 = NO						
35							

Column A (vertical): Names that suggest natural/simple/honest/pure

Sheet1 Sheet2 Sheet3 +

Evidence that we went round the houses before we finally got to a happy
place and called our company innocent

H	I	J	K
es with gin Vodka	Intangible cool factor	Score Max = 14	Other comments
2	2	14	Can't have it
0	2	12	Inferior version to Naked?
2	1	11	Bit unpleasant sounding
2	0	12	Inferior version to Naked?
2	1	13	Good, but still legal problems
2	1	13	My favourite
2	1	13	Less good version of Native
2	0	12	Obvious difficulties and a bit lame
2	1	13	Good, potentially a bit 'aromatherapy'
2	1	10	Good, but shoes have same attitude as us
2	2	12	Definition is 'natural, unaffected and simple'
1	0	8	Sounds like low fat chocolate
2	1	10	Like the idea of Easy/Lazy fruit
2	0	8	Too M&S
1	1	8	Not bad, but a little bit too street
2	1	9	OK, but Wagamamas
2	1	11	Q. Nice
1	1	8	Q.Nice
2	1	10	OK, but Wagamamas
2	1	10	OK, but Wagamamas
0	1	7	Definition is 'a secret medecine'
1	2	11	I like for some reason
2	2	14	Good, but gag could wear thin
1	2	11	I like for some reason
2	1	10	Q. kooky
1	2	12	Bit random but could do a big Jamaican thing
2	1	11	Not quite right

2. Look good

In simple terms, your packaging sells your product the first time, whereas the taste/experience of the product sells it the next hundred times. So in marketing terms the second most important thing to get right after the actual product is the way it is packaged.

In developing our packaging, we were again led by our brand promise and the aim of communicating how natural our drinks were. At that time, all fruit juice was sold in opaque plastic bottles with shiny labels that had pictures of fruit on them. This was because the from-concentrate juice looked murky and 'cooked', and an opaque bottle would hide this less than attractive liquid. This also meant you needed to show pictures of fruit on the label so people would know what was inside.

We didn't have that problem. Our smoothies were made with fresh fruit and had a more vibrant colour. This was a big benefit, and one worth showing off. A see-through bottle was chosen. And because the bottle was clear and people could see in, there was no need to put generic pictures of fruit on the label. Instead, it created an opportunity to do something more distinctive.

At this point, we were working with a design agency called Deepend. We had originally gone to see them in the search for office space as they had some spare. Although living together was not to be, we got on well with the founders, and ended up working with the agency on various bits and pieces.

The main designer was a guy called Gravy. We wanted a simple logo that went with the word innocent – Jon suggested a face with a halo over it. Gravy said 'What, like this?', grabbed a felt tip pen and scrawled a thick outline of a face with two eyes, below a wonky halo. We looked at it and replied, 'Exactly.' So following months of trying, after three seconds with Gravy we'd got the innocent logo sorted. Thanks, Gravy.

The original innocent smoothie label:

innocent©
fresh fruit smoothie

cranberries & raspberries

Not everyone understood what our logo was. A lot of people said,
'We like your juice, but why have you got a drawing of a pig's nose and
a baguette on the front of your bottle?'

Jon took that original sketch and put it straight onto the front of the
label. It was nothing if not simple. But we liked that; simple suggested
that the contents had not been interfered with, and meant the label
quietly stood out on the shelves whereas everyone else's 'shouted'
with bright brash packaging.

The third decision was getting the label paper right. It sounds like a
small thing but everyone else used a shiny plastic paper, and to us it
looked both cheap and artificial. We found an untreated paper that
had bumps and imperfections in it, but was more natural as a result.
Although the supplier said it wouldn't work in the chiller cabinet, tests
in our kitchen and fridge back home meant we felt confident enough
to give it a go. And another lesson was learnt; don't always believe
people who say things won't work.

As the packaging took shape, and all the typical elements needed
on a label were put in place (such as the ingredients and the
nutritional panel), it became clear there was a gap left on the back.

Natural & Perishable
Keep very cold
Shake very hard
Drink very quickly
a fresh product

Ingredients (minimum contents)
2 pressed apples,
½ crushed mango,
1 freshly squeezed orange,
½ mashed banana
2 plump aua*
and 1 crushed passion fruit.

Nutritional Information (per 100ml)
Energy 232KJ (55 Kcal)
Protein 0.4 g
Carbohydrates 12.8 g
of which sugars 11.7 g
Fat 0.7 g
Fibre 0.5 g
Vitamin C 23 mg
Innocent 100 %

This bottle provides
95% RDA of natural Vitamin C
*please forgive us

250ml℮

innocent®
fresh fruit smoothie

mangoes & passion fruits

Now millennium, new world religion; cast aside your infidel carbonated sugar solutions; burn chemical-riddled energy drinks at the stake; proclaim concentrated juices as heretics.

At innocent we religiously believe in the purity of our smoothies - that's why we don't allow anyone or anything to deflower, defame or defile our treasured fruit. And we manage to squeeze ⅓lb of it into each bottle, giving you a day's worth of vitamin C, which is nothing short of a miracle.

Hallelujah.

Why not say hello?
Drop a line or pop around to Fruit Towers,
6 The Buspace, Conlan Street, London W10 5AP

Call the banana phone on 020 8969 7080 or visit our online gym at www.beinnocent.co.uk

® = Religious-experience

---

innocent smoothie
For use-by date see cap.
Keep refrigerated 0-5C.
Gently pasteurised, like milk.
Do the Shake and Vac.*

250ml℮ 0306 1

Ingredients
2½ pressed apples,
6 crushed strawberries (25%),
½ mashed banana (24%),
and a dash of fresh orange juice.

Nutritional Information (per 100ml)
Energy 227kJ (54 kcal)
Protein 0.4 g
Carbohydrates 12 g
Fat 0.5 g
Vitamin C 41 mg (68% RDA per 100 ml)

This bottle provides at least
150% RDA of natural Vitamin C.

1 x 🍌 = YOUR RECOMMENDED DAILY INTAKE OF FRUIT

*and put the freshness back

innocent®
pure fruit smoothie

strawberries & bananas

We're having a bit of a do and we want you to come. It was originally going to be a cheese and wine evening round at Adam's but he's just had a new carpet laid. So we thought that this year we'd put on a big festival and call it Fruitstock. It's free, and it's going to happen on Gloucester Green (in Regents Park, London) on 9th & 10th August. We're going to have lots of live jazz, funk and hip-hop, so you can sit on the grass in the sunshine, listen to some music and share a picnic with your gran or whoever. Looking forward to seeing you there.
What is an innocent smoothie?
A blend of crushed whole fruit, pure and fresh juices and absolutely nothing else.

Bored? Call the banana phone on 020 8600 3939, visit www.fruitstock.com or pop round to say hello to us all at innocent, Fruit Towers, 3 Goldhawk Estate, London W6 0BA

© = Carpet

---

innocent smoothie
For use-by date see cap.
Keep refrigerated 0-5C.
Gently pasteurised, like milk.
Shake before opening.*

250ml℮ 0306 5

Ingredients
2 pressed apples,
½ mashed banana,
11 crushed blackberries (20%),
43 crushed blueberries (11%)
and a dash of fresh orange juice.

Nutritional Information (per 100ml)
Energy 206kJ (48kcal)
Protein 0.6 g
Carbohydrates 11.5 g
Fat 0.1 g
Vitamin C 42 mg (70% RDA per 100 ml)

This bottle provides at least
150% RDA of natural Vitamin C.

1 x 🍌 = YOUR RECOMMENDED DAILY INTAKE OF FRUIT

*not after

innocent®
pure fruit smoothie

blackberries & blueberries

We don't quite know how to go about telling you this. But we are kind of getting into the idea of naturism i.e. living life the natural way, without clothes. We think it would feel liberating to go about your everyday business without a stitch, do the ironing, go to the post office and climb the odd mountain, nude, free and very naked. Obviously, there are certain prejudices against public nudity, but if enough of us do it, it should be fine. Please email your name and details to naturistsallwelcome@innocentdrinks.co.uk and we'll get you involved when the day arrives.
What is an innocent smoothie?
A blend of crushed whole fruit, pure and fresh juices and absolutely nothing else.

Bored? Call the banana phone on 020 8600 3939, visit www.innocentdrinks.co.uk or pop round to say hello to us all at innocent, Fruit Towers, 3 Goldhawk Estate, London W6 0BA

© = Chilly

Natural & Perishable
For use-by date see cap.
Keep refrigerated.
Shake very hard.
Drink very quickly.
a fresh product

Ingredients (minimum contents)
2 pressed apples,
½ mashed banana,
11 crushed raspberries,
50 crushed cranberries,
1 box of chocolate*
and a dash of fresh orange juice.

Nutritional Information (per 100ml)
Energy 176kJ (41kcal)
Protein 0.5 g
Carbohydrates 9.5 g
of which sugars 8.9 g
Fat 0.2 g
Fibre 0.2 g
Sodium 11 mg
Vitamin C 42 mg

This bottle provides
150% RDA of natural Vitamin C
*sorry mum

250ml℮

innocent™
fresh fruit smoothie

cranberries & raspberries

My mum's started buying our smoothies (and that's after a whole year, the skinflint).

I've got to believe and not say anything too rude or controversial. So, mum, they are really good for you. They are made with 100% pure fresh fruit. They contain loads of vitamin C (a day and a half's worth). They are as fat-free as an apple or banana, and that's because they are just fruit. Is that good enough for you mum?

Right, I'm off to smash some windows and have a fag.

Why not say hello?
Drop a line or pop round to Fruit Towers,
Shepherds Bush, London, W6 0BA

Call the banana phone on 020 8600 3939 or visit www.beinnocent.co.uk

TM = Tight Mum

Some of our favourite labels...

Label 1 — pineapples, bananas & coconuts

Ingredients
½ a crushed pineapple (43%),
1 mashed banana (35%),
½ a pressed apple,
some creamy coconut milk (7%),
1 garden shed*
and a dash of freshly squeezed orange juice.

Nutritional info (per 100ml)
Energy 320kJ (76kcal)
Protein 0.7g
Carbohydrate 15.5g
Fat 1.4g
Vitamin C 29mg
(48% RDA per 100ml)

2 LOVELY PORTIONS OF PURE AND FRESH FRUIT
NEVER, EVER, EVER FROM CONCENTRATE
AN INNOCENT SMOOTHIE IS A BLEND OF WHOLE FRUIT, COCONUT MILK, PURE AND FRESH JUICES AND NOTHING ELSE

120% RDA OF NATURAL VITAMIN C

Look after your smoothie
Keep refrigerated 0-5°C before and after opening. Once opened consume within 2 days. For use-by date see cap. Gently pasteurised, like milk. Shake it up baby.

250ml e 0505 1
*I can't find the potting compost

Innocent smoothies contain only the purest and freshest fruit. No concentrates, preservatives or additives of any kind. And they're made and delivered daily. Now that's out of the way I'm using the rest of this space for a personal message: Brian, if you're reading this, do you want to come to the zoo next Thursday? My boss is on a training thing, so it's all cool. They've opened the new penguin bit and apparently one of the pandas is expecting. I've taped this wing mirror to a stick so you don't have to stand on a box or wear those tall shoes or anything. Call me.

An innocent promise
We promise that anything innocent will always taste good and do you good. We promise that we'll never use concentrates, preservatives, stabilisers, or any weird stuff in our drinks. And we promise to always wipe our feet.

Pop round to Fruit Towers, 3 Goldhawk Estate, London W6 0BA, visit www.innocentdrinks.co.uk, e-mail hello@innocentdrinks.co.uk or call the banana phone on 020 8600 3993.

This bottle is made from 25% recycled plastic. We're working on the rest.

innocent
pure fruit smoothie
pineapples, bananas & coconuts

Label 2 — oranges, bananas & pineapples

Ingredients
1 freshly squeezed orange (30%),
½ of a pressed pineapple (30%),
½ a mashed banana (25%),
1 pressed apple
and a dash of lemon juice.

Nutritional info (per 100ml)
Energy 243kJ (57kcal)
Protein 0.6g
Carbohydrate 14.1g
Fat less than 0.1g
Vitamin C 41mg
(68% RDA per 100ml)

2 LOVELY PORTIONS OF PURE AND FRESH FRUIT
NEVER, EVER, EVER FROM CONCENTRATE
AN INNOCENT SMOOTHIE IS A BLEND OF CRUSHED FRUIT, PURE AND FRESH JUICES AND NOTHING ELSE

OVER 170% RDA OF NATURAL VITAMIN C

Look after your smoothie
Keep refrigerated 0-5°C before and after opening. Once opened consume within 2 days. For use-by date see cap. Gently pasteurised, like milk. Shake it up baby.

250ml e 0508 5

Do you remember when you used to go round to your mate's house and be envious of their family? Their mum was really cool and spoke to you like a grown up. They ate really great modern food, like pizza and chicken kievs. And the dad listened to Pink Floyd and relaxed in the evening with long, hand-rolled cigarettes. So cool. We want our innocent family to be like this. And we reckon it is. A bit. Join us at www.innocentdrinks.co.uk/family. Mini kievs are on us.

An innocent promise
We promise that anything innocent will always taste good and do you good. We promise that we'll never use concentrates, preservatives, stabilisers, or any weird stuff in our drinks. And if we do you can tell our Mums.

Pop round to Fruit Towers, 3 Goldhawk Estate, London W6 0BA, visit www.innocentdrinks.co.uk, e-mail hello@innocentdrinks.co.uk or call the banana phone on 020 8600 3993.

This bottle is made from 25% recycled plastic. We're working on the rest.

innocent
pure fruit smoothie
oranges, bananas & pineapples

Label 3 — pineapples, bananas & coconuts

3 GOOD REASONS TO DRINK THIS SMOOTHIE
1. THERE ARE 2 PORTIONS OF FRUIT IN EVERY BOTTLE
2. IT PROVIDES 13% OF YOUR GDA OF FIBRE
3. IT GIVES YOU THE GOODNESS OF 5 DIFFERENT TYPES OF FRUIT

PLEASE KEEP ME COLD
This smoothie must be kept refrigerated between 0-5°C before and after opening. Once opened consume within 2 days. For use-by date see cap. Gently pasteurised, like milk. Shake it up baby.

AN INNOCENT SMOOTHIE IS A BLEND OF CRUSHED FRUIT, COCONUT MILK & PURE JUICES

Ingredients
½ a pressed gold pineapple (43%),
1 mashed banana (35%),
½ a pressed apple,
some creamy coconut milk (7%),
a squeeze of orange
and a dash of lemon.

Nutritional info (per 100ml)
Energy 292kJ (69kcal)
Protein 0.8g
Carbohydrate 14.9g
(of which sugars†) 12.9g
Fat 1.3g
(of which saturates) 1g
Fibre 1.2g
Sodium 2mg
Vitamin C 34mg
(57% RDA per 100ml)
†sugars found naturally in the fruit

250ml e FCX039 5

2 portions of fruit

Before horses were invented people had to make do with banging 2 coconut shells together and imagining that a horse was passing by. This was difficult as no one knew what a horse looked like or, more importantly, what a horse was. We should count ourselves lucky as there are plenty of horses to choose from these days. And should you ever want to recreate the experience of a horse in your own home without getting one in, just bang 2 coconut shells together and knock a few things over. Instant horse.

PROMISE #3 SOURCE ETHICALLY
We favour farms with high social and environmental standards, for example working with the Rainforest Alliance to source our bananas responsibly.

Twiddling your thumbs? Pop round to Fruit Towers, 1 Goldhawk Estate, London W6 0BA, e-mail hello@innocentdrinks.com, call the banana phone on 020 8600 3993 (UK) or 01 864 4100 (ROI). Join the family at www.innocentdrinks.com/family

This bottle is made from 50% recycled plastic. Please recycle it so we can make more.

innocent
pure fruit smoothie
pineapples, bananas & coconuts

Other brands' packaging didn't seem to have anything else other than statements such as 'your statutory rights are not affected'. We didn't know what that meant, so we left it off. But that left more room, so the idea came to us to write little stories. The space was essentially a free advert; an opportunity to talk about the drink, the business and other things we wanted to communicate, and if written well, would give people something more interesting to do than watch the person opposite them on the tube pick their nose. And by constantly changing the words and keeping them interesting, it meant people would hopefully read the labels and tell others about them. Over the years it has become the cheapest and most effective way to communicate the brand and what we stand for. Plus we get to make bad jokes and stitch each other up, in print.

3. Be seen in the right places

Where a brand is seen also communicates. Celebrities know this; that's why they make sure they get photographed coming out of the right clubs, rather than down their local Homebase on a Saturday afternoon. And so too for us. Our launch strategy focused on getting our bottles seen in the right places. We called them our beacon outlets, and when we launch in a new country, it's one of the first things we do – get listed in the places that most communicate what we stand for.

First and foremost innocent is a food company that cares deeply about good quality food. And to signal that, we concentrate on getting stocked in the premium food outlets in a city – the food halls of the leading department stores and wonderful delis run by people passionate about food. innocent also stands for health and keeping things natural, so getting stocked in the leading health food shops is important. In London at the time of our launch, Planet Organic and Wild Oats were the leading wholefood shops and were top of our list – we went to see them early on and fortunately they agreed to stock us. And finally, because we like a bit of glitz, we want to be seen in a few hip places too – clubs, posh hotels and fancy shops. Which explains why in the first few months of innocent's life you could find our smoothies in the then recently opened China White nightclub, the café in the DKNY shop on Bond Street and the Met Hotel on Park Lane, as well as backstage during London Fashion Week. (We thought we'd get to meet loads of models when we dropped off the drinks and fridges. But we swiftly learnt that models tend not to talk to people who are delivering fridges.)

4. Get yourself in the papers

PR can make or break a brand. We had an experience within our first few weeks that taught us this. It's a long-winded story, but one worth telling.

After a few days of being in business, Adam returned from a meeting looking disappointed. He'd been trying to sell our drinks into the Harvey Nichols food hall and they had said no. This was bad news: they were at the top of our beacon outlet list. We thought that if we got our drinks in there, it would make it easier to get them in everywhere else. But they said no, and as persuasive as Adam can be, they wouldn't budge.

In an unconnected event, but on the same day, Jon received a request from a friend of his. Would we be happy to be interviewed for a story in the *Evening Standard* about setting up businesses in London? It would really help his girlfriend out. An easy request for us to say yes to.

The journalist did the interview, and a complimentary piece ran the next day, titled 'London's new eco-entrepreneurs'. Unbeknownst to us, a TV producer from LWT read the piece and decided to feature innocent on his TV show, *Capital Gains*. But when he rang directory enquiries to get our number, they didn't have our details. Unperturbed, and by pure coincidence, he called Harvey Nichols, as he assumed that innocent would be sold there. He rang the food hall and asked to speak to the juice buyer, who by luck turned out to be the same person Adam had met with. Introducing himself by saying that he had read about innocent in the papers and that he wanted to feature innocent on his TV show, he asked if Harvey Nichols stocked innocent. The buyer replied that they didn't, but following his call they certainly would.

And so a couple of days after being rejected from one of our most important targets, we got two phone calls in quick succession – one from a producer asking if he could feature us on his TV show and one from Harvey Nichols saying they would like to stock us. That was a good day.

It was an unlikely sequence of events, but it illustrated the effect that PR can have. Even more so than advertising, people are influenced by what they see in the papers and watch on TV. And best of all, it's free.

Although a journalist won't write about something if it isn't interesting or true, it's possible to increase the chances of your story getting picked up by the press. If you read the papers you'll find features where businesses and brands are written about on a regular basis. There may be a product page where goods like yours are reviewed. Or a regular interview slot with a new budding entrepreneur (the *Sunday Times* business section features one every week). Make a note of the name of the journalist. Ring the paper and ask to speak to them. Explain that you've read their story and would like you/your business/your products to be considered next time they're writing that type of piece. Send them some samples. And a short press release, explaining what you do. Tell them what's interesting about your business – maybe you started it with friends or your product is made by a wizard who lives in a cave. Whatever is different and relevant and true. If the story's interesting and you've pitched it to the right person, you'll find most journalists will be glad that you got in touch, and you may get to see yourself in print. And that first bit of coverage will do wonders when trying to persuade your customers/employees/ mum that you just might be onto something.

People are quitting highly-paid, successful careers to start new businesses of their own. But this time with a social conscience attached. **EMILY SHEFFIELD** met some of London's eco-entrepreneurs

All Innocent good fun: "We've always wanted to work for ourselves. We had to do it or shut up," say Jon Wright, Adam Balon and Richard Reed

Boys just want to have fun...

WHEN Adam Balon, Jon Wright and Richard Reed quit lucrative jobs to start their own company, their incomes slumped — but there were compensations. "We've cleaned ourselves out financially," says Balon. "It might have caused sleepless nights and panic attacks, but we've laughed a lot."

Aged only 27, they have started a fresh-fruit drink company called Fresh. Each deserted lucrative careers in marketing, management consultancy and advertising; Wright was so keen to begin he quit one month short of a £10,000 bonus.

"We've always wanted to work for ourselves. We either had to do it or shut up," says Reed, whose ad campaign involves persuading nuns to hand out the company's smoothies "to promote its purity". The boys, all firm friends, felt they had got to a threshold in their careers. "It was knuckle down or try something new," explains Wright. "And we love our smoothies, it's not all cynical marketing." Their drinks, named Innocent, were first sold at their local café off Ladbroke Grove three weeks ago: "We crept past late Friday night, peering in to see if they'd sold well — they had. It reduced our paranoia only slightly. Now we sell to 60 outlets," says Reed.

Juice is a booming area for would-be entrepreneurs. Tim Scott, recently ended a 10-year stint in the City and opened a juice bar: "I took a long, hard look at what I'd achieved and realised I was unhappy with what I'd been doing. OK, I've spent the money and had great fun but the trade-off was not great." Seven weeks ago he opened Fluid, on the Fulham Road, the result of a "whole change in my life ... I'd lunched and drunk too much for years. I joined a gym and went to California. I saw all these juice bars and thought it was a concept I could adapt for London. I felt if it was a lifestyle issue for me, it could be for others."

This time last year Alison Rose, 30, and her husband, Tony Guy, 34, were a high-flying media couple. She was a presenter for Australian Sky News, he a successful TV executive producer. They had an enviable lifestyle: beautiful apartment overlooking Sydney Harbour, swimming pool, large expense accounts, and combined earnings of £100,000. But

last March they left their jobs, sold their flat, gave their cats away and flew thousands of miles to London. Their new office is a damp basement in Paddington, their home a cramped flat in west Kensington and they risk losing their life-savings. And for what? "We didn't want to work in a corporation anymore. We wanted to have our own company, to do something we believed in," says Rose. "We saw there was a gap in the market for low-fat cafés and this became our obsession." That dream is now manifested in Luscious, London's

first low-fat café. "We're earning less and the stress has been enormous," she adds, puffing on a roll-up in their messy basement in Praed Street, W2, "but we are in control of our lives."

You may think their actions capricious, even cuckoo (sunny Sydney for London?), but they are among a swelling group of successful careerists who reach the top, only to trade it all in to start their own companies. And they're not choosing any old money-spinning schemes — these are painted a fashionable green. So you have City boys setting

up juice bars, music executives publicising complementary health companies and car salesmen making organic pizzas. They're not eco-warriors but they're doing their bit while filling their coffers. It's Sixties-idealism-meets-Nineties capitalism. In Peter Mandelson-speak, it's business for the new millennium.

"Timing was paramount," continues Rose. "We had no kids and we thought if we didn't do it now we never would." Guy agrees: "In your twenties there seems so much time ahead, but in your thirties you realise you have to take responsibility for your future. We didn't want to be on our death beds regretting what we didn't do. We follow a low-fat diet and we're trying to educate others."

Their friends, entrepreneurs Jeremy Jaffé and Rolf Depolla, used to sell cars. Now they run What on Earth, an organic pizza company based in Battersea. "It was difficult selling cars when you are moderate eco-bunnies," explains 35-year-old Jaffé. "Money was the carrot with cars, now it's healthy living. Both of us were bored with what we were doing so we thought, why not?" Their office is a desk surrounded by pizza ovens, sacks of herbs, tomatoes and fresh dough. A couple of men in white overalls and What on Earth T-shirts are diligently assembling pizzas. "We wanted to do something organic. If we were going to give up comforts, we had to do something worthwhile. We didn't want to be just another company selling rubbish," says Depolla, also 35. Their customer hot-list now includes Harvey Nichols, Wild Oats, the Fresh Food Company and Planet Organic. "Setting up your own business is very stressful but more fulfilling," finishes Jaffé. "And we're proud of what we're selling. But 10 years from now, when we've made enough money, we'll retire to Rolf's eco-house in Costa Rica.

NO matter how long you've been in your job — or how far up the ladder you've risen — the bug can still bite. Ruth Katz spent 21 years climbing the corporate rungs of the music industry before she decided things had to change. "For the last eight years in the music industry I was a vice president at EMI. I worked so hard I made myself ill," she admits. Katz, now 38, says yoga, acupuncture and pilates helped her cope and was the inspiration for her new company, the Complementary Group, a business management company for those involved in alternative medicine and therapy. "I realised my values were shifting away from the music industry where the bottom line is money. Roles have to change otherwise people and their work becomes stale," she says. "This is a new passion developed through personal experience. I'm told I look younger, I feel alive and my time is my own."

The eco-entrepreneurs have landed: from left, Tony Guy, Alison Rose, Jeremy Jaffé, Ruth Katz and Rolf Depolla; right, juice "tycoon" Tim Scott

The newspaper article that got us stocked in Harvey Nichols. *Evening Standard*, 27 May 1999

'And for a limited period, madam, each drink comes with a free hand-knitted toy'

If your product's good, then there's no greater advert than having someone try it. The person who knew this more than anyone was William Wrigley Jnr, the founder of Wrigley's gum. In 1915, he sent four free sticks of his gum to every person listed in the phone books of America. As a result he captured 50% of the American gum market overnight, which Wrigley's have retained to this day. Nice work, William Jnr.

Wrigley's gum – it used to be free but now it costs about 37p

Unfortunately, our smoothies don't post so well, but right from the outset we let people sample them in the shops where we were sold. This involved us setting up a little table and giving away a taster – if people liked it they could buy some from the shop. Slightly reminiscent of a drug dealer's tactics, but in this case, a bit healthier.

Sampling face to face with your drinker also creates an opportunity to tell people about your product and, most importantly, hear what they think about the drink and the company. That's useful; as the motivational posters testify, feedback is the breakfast of champions. Plus it tells you if you need more pork in your pie, or whatever it is you're selling.

As always, the basic rule remains the same – everything communicates, especially the person giving out the samples. Some brands use their front line staff to carve out a real point of difference. For example, MAC cosmetics in the States deliberately recruit nontraditional team members to man their stands in the conservative cosmetic halls of the department stores of New York and LA – women with piercings, tattoos and other body art; gay men in great shape; trannies in drag. All to make a more edgy, left-of-centre statement about the brand.

So check that your ambassadors represent whatever it is you want to communicate. Check that they know their onions, and care about them too – they're the first person from your business that a particular consumer is ever going to meet. First impressions last.

6. Go digital

Harnessing the power of digital media is a brilliant way to establish a brand. President Obama understood this clearly. His election campaign was the ultimate marketing strategy. (A simple clear promise – 'Change'. A product that credibly represented it – himself. Even a great endline – 'Yes we can'.) But the campaign's most distinctive feature was the use of digital media to recruit and engage directly with a countrywide multi-generational army of voters and participants. By election time he had the email addresses of 13 million supporters, cash donations via his website from 3 million of them, 2 million profiles on his own social networking site and 1.2 million active community volunteers. A reservoir of support simply unimaginable and untappable before the advent of digital media, and which helped deliver him his historic majority.

Now, if you're running a business selling chocolate biscuits then the goals and visions you have will most likely be less bold and transformational than Obama's, but they will be important none the less. And the potential of digital media is at your disposal just as much as it was to Obama, to communicate and engage with your potential cash voters and constituents. So you should work it hard. We have benefited from doing so since we started the business.

From the beginning we built a simple website that was easy to update and meant we could change messages, news and information on a daily basis without cost. We printed the web address on our bottles and within the first few weeks received emails from drinkers who wanted to find out more about the company. We offered to email them news once we had any. To our surprise, all eleven of them said yes. The next Monday Dan wrote our first newsletter and emailed it to them, keeping them up to date with important events, such as the time Richard was found hopping around the office with a flaming bin stuck on the end of his leg, after he'd tried to stomp out a minor fire in it.

Thus began what we now call 'the innocent family' – a group of people who quite like hearing what we are up to, who get our news emailed to them every week and to send a little gift to once in a while. The family is now 120,000 people strong, having grown from the original eleven.

Nowadays we also have a blog, films on YouTube, plenty of Flickr groups, Facebook fans, Twitter feeds and whatever else we can have a go at. The trick for us has been to try all of these things without pinning much hope on any particular one as the future of marketing as we know it. Instead, they're all just new ways in which we can have conversations with people. We like conversations, because they're two-way and if they're good, you learn stuff. Basically, if there's a new way in which our drinkers want to communicate with us, then we'll get involved.

7. And then advertise

It took until the sixth year of business before we started investing materially in advertising. Our plan was always to do it last, once the brand was distributed and established. This was partly out of necessity (we couldn't afford it to begin with) and partly by design: the product, the packaging and the grass roots activities we've outlined above allowed us to get noticed in a way that built a certain authenticity for the brand among early adopters. But once we got stocked in supermarkets it became clear there was an opportunity to tell more people about innocent smoothies and introduce them to the brand.

our digital world

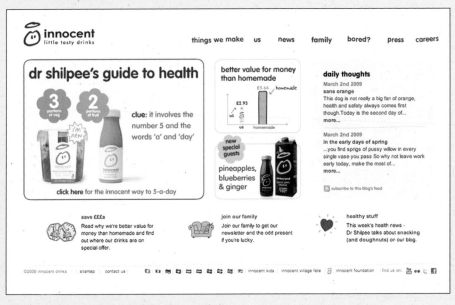

It began with our website. Simple, clean and clear

Then we started experimenting, with our blog, Twitter and a little bit of Flickr

the innocent news

4th February 2009

Ready? Sitting comfortably? Needle and thread at the ready? Right then..."Snow news is good news." Ho ho. Guffaw. Now please sew your sides back up and let's get on with it.

All white now

This week got off to a funny start. Monday wasn't rubbish, it wasn't brilliant, it was just sort of all white (sorry). Yes, it snowed, right out of the sky, just like in the movies. About 30 of us managed to plough through it, get to the office and then spent most of our morning lunchbreak blindsiding respected colleagues with high velocity iceballs, building snowmen and planning where to sleep in case we got blizzarded in. We posted our snowman art on the blog and lots of you did the same, so we thought we'd make a little competition of it. Check out three generations of snow people here, upload your snow sculpture photos here and our top 3 favourites will win an extra chilled box of our finest.

Masterchef – it could be you

We like Masterchef. And we're still trying to work out which incarnation we like best. Is it Loyd Grossman, with his colour coded kitchens and considered judgments? Or is it Greg and John's "I'd quite happily put my face in it" current version of the show? The jury is out, but we thought it would be good to have a go ourselves, so here you are. We challenge you to become our Veg Pot Chef of the Year, and we'll try to convince Greg or John (or maybe even Loyd) to pop down to judge. Maybe. All you have to do is follow the instructions here in this blog post – then we'll pick our best three chefs, get them into Fruit Towers and let battle commence. Click here if you fancy having a go.

Our man in Kenya

30 something, slightly pasty, IT professional with strong Wolverhampton accent. WLT travel, learn and help where he can. Not a classified from The Dudley Evening News but a decent description of our JT who is currently out in Kenya. He's working with Excellent Development, one of the NGOs that the innocent foundation supports, helping them with their IT systems and seeing for himself the work that they do. Being good with computers and that, he's posting regular updates on the blog while he's out there – follow his progress here.

Are you one of the eleven?

It's a long shot but it just might work. We're looking for the eleven people who first received our news in email form, back in Autumn 1999. If you think you're one of them, please email our Dan. Thank you very much.

And finally...

- The immortal jellyfish.
- Grassy trams.
- Snowing for broke.
- How to use the internets.
- Watermelon art.
- Stay clear of poison.

Our weekly email newsletter

And the wonderful world of our Facebook group

As usual, we started small. In fact, our first advertising campaign consisted of a mere five billboards (we rather cheekily just put posters up outside the head offices of the major supermarkets in the hope they would notice us and think the campaign was bigger than it was). The next year we did a proper London wide poster campaign, and the following year the same thing nationally.

We did our first TV campaign in 2005, with an ad we wrote ourselves and got a friend to film on a video camera in the Park just around the corner from Fruit Towers. It was simple if nothing else, and featured our carton waddling on to the screen, with fruit appearing and disappearing to the sounds of pings and pops. It cost less than £5000 to make and while we have subsequently made more expensive ads, it is still the most effective ad we've ever run.

Now that's what we call marketing.

Our low-cost approach to the dark arts of marketing

1. *Make (and keep) a promise*

2. *Choose the right stage name*

3. *Look good*

4. *Be seen in the right places*

5. *Get yourself in the papers*

6. *Give it away*

7. *Go digital*

8. *And then advertise*

When we finally had enough money to make adverts, this is what we did.
This one's from 2003

Nature's way of keeping you healthy. And the reason you've never seen a monkey on a rowing machine.

innocent smoothies. nothing but nothing but fruit.

This one's from 2006. It's the first time we managed to mention a monkey in our ads

how to make an innocent smoothie

squeeze one of these

over lots of these

wait for a bit

nearly there

bingo

nothing but nothing but fruit
and a nice long sleep in a field

And this is from summer 2006

Here's a shot from our January 2007 TV ad. We were on a budget so we got Dan to feature in it

innocent smoothies. innocent by nature.

And another from a TV slot we ran in January 2008 with a voiceover from none other than Johnny Ball

chapter eight
take care of
the details

Take care of the details

By its very nature, business is competitive. Irrespective of whether you are big, small, new or old, you'll be up against competitors with good products, a strong brand, great distribution and better biscuits in the meeting room. And if you want to compete, you'll have to beat them at some or all of these things, and then keep beating them. That's the bad news. The good news is that once you've got all the big things sorted, it is surprising how the small details can be used to help you win.

When Virgin Atlantic give out ice cream in the middle of the in-flight movie, when howies put a 'free water' tap in the middle of their clothing store, when Cape Clear, our local fishmonger in Shepherd's Bush, give out fresh herbs and lemon when you buy a nice piece of fish, they're all using details to do what details do best: giving us consumers a story to tell, and maybe even a reason to buy there again.

Since the day we started innocent we've focused on the details. From the words on the labels to the vans we drive around in, from the blurb on our blog to the way we decorate Fruit Towers, we've always tried to go big on the small stuff.

No single little idea is significant in its own right, but if you have enough of them they may add up to something bigger, especially if there is commonality and consistency between them. That's why as well as having lots of little ideas, it's also important to have a tone and a sense of personality – a way of speaking and a feeling that holds the cobweb of little ideas together, which creates a greater whole.

Own a tone

Our innocent tone and approach come from the fact that we're a company started by friends. We talk to each other and our consumers in the way we talk to our friends (minus the swear words). It is not insincere; it's an attempt to encourage a natural, warm, open and consistent way of communicating. Plus, the 'talk as friends' principle stops us taking ourselves too seriously.

We now judge decisions, ideas and our choice of words against whether they feel 'innocent' or not. It has become an adjective to describe whether something adds to, or subtracts from, the brand. We recognise that this is self-referential, so rather than slowly disappear up our own backsides while trying to explain it, we'd rather show some examples of our little ideas and our tone, instead of trying to theorise too hard.

Label details

We realised early on that food labelling could be quite dull. So as well as writing the stories for the back we also popped in the odd comedy ingredient, just to make our labels a slightly more interesting read.

This approach has not been without its complications. After a few months of selling drinks, we got a letter from the Trading Standards Officer (TSO) at our local council. She had spotted the addition of '2 plump nuns' to the ingredients panel on one of our labels (see page 120). We apologised, and explained it was just a joke hinting at the purity of our drinks. The TSO said it wasn't allowed and that consumers could get confused. We said we thought it unlikely that people would buy the drink expecting to find two nuns in it, or be disappointed when they couldn't find them. But the TSO didn't agree and proceeded to launch an official enquiry. This rumbled on for several weeks, and involved us being summoned for formal interviews and legal consultations. The end result of the enquiry: us being sent a letter that stated the immortal lines: 'you must either remove the reference to "plump nuns" on your labels or start putting them in your fruit juice'. To this day it remains the best letter we've ever received.

Most of the little details on the labels have a story behind them. For example, on the usage instructions we sometimes write 'Shake before opening (not after)'. This came from the time Jon walked into Fruit Towers with smoothie all down his T-shirt. He explained he'd been sat

We realised early on that we could do what we wanted on the back of our packs, so we try to make it interesting

Carton 1

please keep me in the fridge and shake* me before pouring

the soul of a fruit

So, you thought a good banana was easily recognisable? Yellow, bendy, no big bruises? Maybe so, but can you see into the banana's soul? We believe we can. It's a gift that was given to us at a fairground long ago. And it's why we work with the Rainforest Alliance, who employ great people like Carlos. His job is to check all our bananas have been grown with respect for local biodiversity, by farms who protect the surrounding rainforests and by farmers who are treated and paid fairly for their work. Oh yes. Those bananas have got soul.

fancy a chat?

Us too. Just pop in to Fruit Towers, 1 Goldhawk Estate, Brackenbury Road, London, W6 0BA or ring the banana phone on 020 8600 3993. In Ireland, visit us at Fruit Towers, 46 Mountjoy Square, Dublin 1 or call 01 864 4100. Otherwise email doormat@innocentdrinks.com, or even join the family at www.innocentdrinks.com/family

Carton 2

please keep me in the fridge and shake* me before pouring

pounds of fruit

Hard maths – simultaneous quadratic equations, advanced trigonometry and getting stabbed with a compass.

Simple maths – this carton of smoothie is better value than the sum of buying all the fruit yourself, making it at home and then having to do the washing up afterwards.

For those of you who like equations, here's one for you:

$$f + b + w = z$$
$$i = a$$

key:
f = cost of fruit
b = blender hunt
w = wrinkly hands
z = less value
i = innocent carton
a = better value

For those of you who are more visual types, here's a nice picture to illustrate:

And for those of you who like small dogs in jumpers, this one's for you:

fancy a chat?

Us too. Just pop in to Fruit Towers, 1 Goldhawk Estate, Brackenbury Road, London, W6 0BA or ring the banana phone on 020 8600 3993. In Ireland, visit us at Fruit Towers, 46 Mountjoy Square, Dublin 1 or call 01 864 4100. Otherwise email doormat@innocentdrinks.com, or even join the family at www.innocentdrinks.com/family

Carton 3

please keep me in the fridge and shake* me before pouring

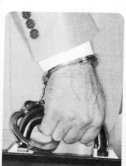

The Cosa Nostra

There's a reason why this recipe tastes so very good. And it's a big fat secret. But since you asked...we're very specific about the mangoes we use and the exact moment when they're ripe enough to crush. A day either way is a day too wrong. But our growers have signed special forms. They've sworn an oath. We'll never tell and neither will they. So trust us, these secrets are for your drinking benefit. Don't try to find out too much; accidents will happen. Capiche?

fancy a chat?

Us too. Just pop in to Fruit Towers, 1 Goldhawk Estate, Brackenbury Road, London, W6 0BA or ring the banana phone on 020 8600 3993. In Ireland, visit us at Fruit Towers, 46 Mountjoy Square, Dublin 1 or call 01 864 4100. Otherwise email doormat@innocentdrinks.com, or even join the family at www.innocentdrinks.com/family

please keep me in the fridge and shake* me before pouring

*it helps if the cap's on

STAR JUMPS

TURBO

Staying healthy is a serious business. Admittedly, it can be hard to stay serious when you're squeezed into Lycra leggings, backside bouncing, doing turbo star jumps in a turbo star jump class. However, if you prefer your health to come carton-shaped, please let us help.

This recipe contains only 110 calories per 250ml serving, whilst providing you with 23% of your daily fibre. And all you have to do is gulp. No Lycra, no unsightly bulging, no sweat. Please enjoy.

fancy a chat?
Us too. Just pop in to Fruit Towers, 1 Goldhawk Estate, Brackenbury Road, London, W6 0BA or ring the banana phone on 020 8600 3993. In Ireland, visit us at Fruit Towers, 46 Mountjoy Square, Dublin 1 or call 01 864 4100. Otherwise email doormat@innocentdrinks.com, or even join the family at www.innocentdrinks.com/family

---

please keep me in the fridge and shake* me before pouring

*it helps if the cap's on

drink in colour

Variety is the spice of life. And we believe in variety. Importantly, so do nutritional experts, who say that we should be eating lots of different types of fruit and veg, in order to get a whole spectrum of vitamins, goodness and whatnot. So you can guess the next bit – innocent smoothies are made from a wide variety of fruit. Each glassful contains at least five different types of fruit. Really. So, please drink up.

fancy a chat?
Us too. Just pop in to Fruit Towers, 1 Goldhawk Estate, Brackenbury Road, London, W6 0BA or ring the banana phone on 020 8600 3993. In Ireland, visit us at Fruit Towers, 46 Mountjoy Square, Dublin 1 or call 01 864 4100. Otherwise email doormat@innocentdrinks.com, or even join the family at www.innocentdrinks.com/family

---

please keep me in the fridge and shake* me before pouring

*it helps if the cap's on

fig.1   fig.2   fig.3

knees please

Bees are good at lots of stuff. Flying, pollinating, making honey, keeping small children on their toes. But they are never the bee's knees. Nothing is in fact. Because bees do not possess knees. Saying someone is 'the bee's knees' is as odd as saying they're 'the donkey's driving license' or the 'owl's tax return form'.

Not that we want you to stop complimenting people, mind. We just don't want you to make a fool of yourself. So next time you're dishing out the compliments, remember to say something is 'the bee's legs'. Fact based, yet still complimentary.

fig.1 Not a knee

fig.2 Also not a knee

fig.3 A knee? Nope

fancy a chat?
Us too. Just pop in to Fruit Towers, 1 Goldhawk Estate, Brackenbury Road, London, W6 0BA or ring the banana phone on 020 8600 3993. In Ireland, visit us at Fruit Towers, 46 Mountjoy Square, Dublin 1 or call 01 864 4100. Otherwise email doormat@innocentdrinks.com, or even join the family at www.innocentdrinks.com/family

on the bus coming into work after a heavy night before, and shaken up the smoothie he was about to start drinking. The only issue being in his hungover state he'd forgotten he'd already removed the cap.

The line 'Separation may sometimes occur (but mummy still loves daddy)' has proved controversial to some people over the years, and has led to several emails of the 'no she bloody doesn't' variety.

Our vans

Our first van was a regular white van, refrigerated to keep the drinks cold. It got bashed up pretty quickly, mainly because Richard wasn't very good at getting through those posts that make the road a bit narrower.

After a while we needed another van, so in a moment of astute business foresight we bought a smaller one to fit through the posts. But again it was white, and in London there are a lot of white vans, which is quite boring. We sat down to figure out how to make our van more interesting and received inspiration from probably the greatest van of all time:

The *Dumb and Dumber* 'Mutt Cutts' van.

Armed with this inspiration, and the fact that we had just started making our first yoghurt-based thickie, we settled on the cow as our beast of choice. This is how they look side by side:

Spot the difference

Features included horns on the roof (excellent for getting stuck in low-ceilinged car parks), a swishy tail and some udders at the back. The search for udders was particularly interesting – we found out quickly that there aren't many different types of fake udders on the market. So in the end we got hold of some teats – the sort used to bottle-feed orphaned calves. They worked a treat when spray-painted pink. But the best bit was the button on the dashboard that, when pressed, made the van emit a loud 'moo'. Driving past a crowd of tourists in Covent Garden? Press the button. Passing a primary school at 3.45pm? Press the button. Spot a pretty girl? Definitely press the button. Twice.

People liked it because they'd never seen one before, and in those early days when we delivered our drinks around London ourselves, our vans were a fine advert for the company, driving round town all day.

Later on, we started covering bigger vans in AstroTurf and made them dance, courtesy of some hydraulic magic. Thus was born the Dancing Grass Van. And we now have smaller grassy vans too. We have definitely been satisfying some daft childlike urges in doing all of this, but then it's kids who always seem to have the most fun.

Our place

We currently have seven offices across Europe. London, Dublin, Paris, Copenhagen, Hamburg, Stockholm and Salzburg. The largest of these is in London, where we started, and is known (to us at least) as Fruit Towers. The 'towers' bit is a little misleading, seeing as it's a low-rise industrial unit in Shepherd's Bush, West London. The original dream was to buy an old tower block and stick a big revolving strawberry on top of it, but we never got round to that.

We've been in our current place since August 2000. We started off with one unit, then got the place next door when we grew, and then did the same again when we grew some more. Nowadays we have six of these units, all merged into one, with lots more desks inside than the seven we originally had when we moved. Our development

The innocent DGV (Dancing Grass Van) and friend

kitchen sits right in the middle – that's the place where recipes get invented and tested – and the whole building is carpeted in AstroTurf, because we always fancied being able to work in a place where you could feel the grass between your toes.

When it comes down to it, Fruit Towers is an office. There are desks and swivel chairs and computers dotted throughout. Lots of work needs to get done. But seeing as we get to choose how it looks and feels, we've tried to add a few innocent touches, which hopefully make it a better place in which to work and talk and get stuff done.

And we've tried to make sure that each of our new offices gets the same treatment – ultimately, an innocent office should be somewhere that you want to go to every morning, and not some grey place that you try to escape from.

'Hello, innocent banana phone...'

Our communal work area. Bad shorts optional

The Bored Room

How big decisions get made

A birthday picnic on the benches

For our shopkeepers

We aim to work the details across every part of our business, including little touches for the good people who stock our drinks. The aim is always to come up with details that will make innocent a better company to deal with, and make people's working day a little easier. Some of the things we've done over the years for our retailers include:

• Gloves for our shelf stackers. The idea came from the observation that people who spend most of their day in and around fridges tend to have cold hands. So why not make them some gloves, with grippy bits to make it easier to carry boxes.

• At Christmas we hid chocolate money in each case of innocent drinks that was delivered to the shops. As well as being a small thank you to the people who actually get our drinks onto shelves, it also meant they were getting our bottles out of their boxes and onto shelves much quicker. Everyone loves free chocolate.

• Pimp my staffroom. A few years ago we all went and spent a day or two working in a supermarket. We learnt lots that day, including the fact that the staffroom is where it all happens. So we ran a competition to pimp a staffroom.

• Original innocent stockist certificate. Created to recognise those who have been stocking our drinks for many a long year.

Again, not massive things, but all of these details hopefully add up.

Free gloves for important people

When details go wrong

The risk you take when trying to make every little thing interesting or amusing is that some of them don't work...

• The Bush Van – we wanted this vehicle to show nature in all its glory, but all we got was a Renault van that looked like it had just returned from a tour in 'Nam (see below).

• Our third birthday invite. The theme was 'down on the innocent farm' and the invite was a small box of straw containing an egg, supposedly hard boiled. However, an uncooked egg was sent to the boss at Sainsbury's, who was away for a fortnight's holiday. Result – a two-week-old raw smashed egg on the desk of our most important customer.

• We bought some posh-looking silver display fridges to put into important outlets. They looked very swish, but it turned out they were better at warming things up than cooling things down. This resulted in fermenting smoothies in two of our most important launch customers (Harvey Nichols and Fresh & Wild). Doh.

If you look carefully you can see a van

Where do ideas come from?

As you can tell, we probably spend more time on the small details than the big decisions. The bigger questions about what country or category to go into next don't come round that often, and you usually figure out these larger decisions if you get the relevant clever people to work it out and do the maths. But the small stuff is tricky. There's no process for creating them. They just have to be thought of by someone, somehow.

It's worth saying that they don't all spring fully formed from someone's brain. We get ideas from a thousand different people and places, a creative process also known as stealing. And we can trace lots of our ideas back to the original source (see overleaf).

Micro Wolf and the four rooms

Our favourite theory for thinking up ideas came from a man called Michael Wolff. Our name for him is Micro Wolf, but that's another story. He set up a seminal branding agency in the '60s called Wolff Olins, which was regarded as one of the best in the world. He talks about the four 'rooms' you should visit when trying to think of original ideas.

The first 'room' is the 'room of great work'. Expose yourself to the best the world has to offer in ideas. Literally visit the art galleries of the world. Spend time in design museums. Read the magazines and the reviews and experience the finest of every art form. Track down whatever is regarded as the best of its kind; be it architecture, technology or the world's greatest teapot. Revel in them. Be inspired by them. But do not do your work in this 'room' as you will find yourself dominated by their greatness, creating a lesser version of what has come before.

Next, visit the 'room of understanding'. Whatever industry you work in, make sure you understand how it works; the fundamental drivers of the way things are. If you are trying to come up with an idea for a

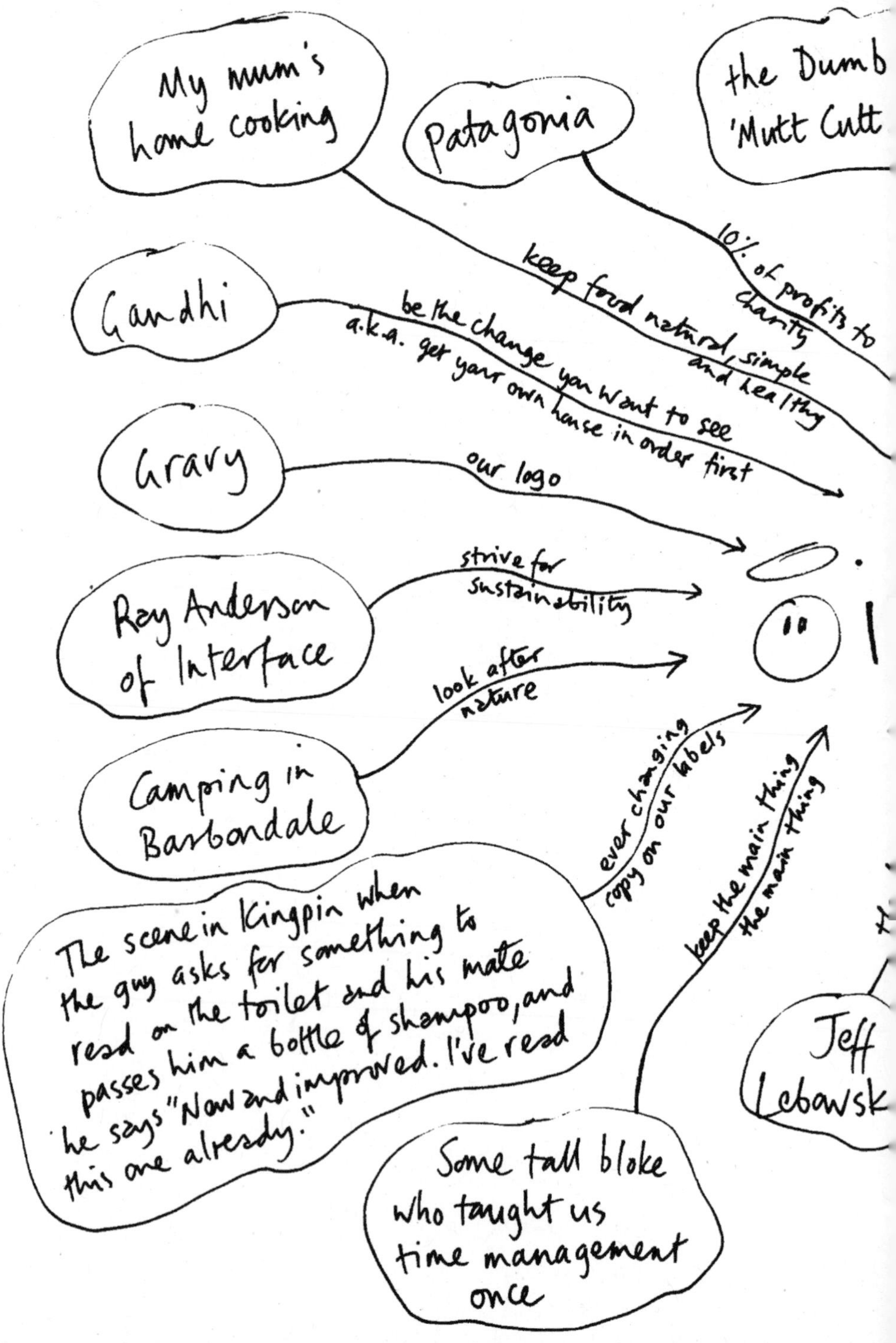

My mum's home cooking

Patagonia

the Dumb 'Mutt Cult

10% of profits to charity

Gandhi

keep food natural, simple and healthy

be the change you want to see
a.k.a. get your own house in order first

Gravy

our logo

Ray Anderson of Interface

strive for sustainability

look after nature

Camping in Barbondale

ever changing copy on our labels

keep the main thing the main thing

The scene in Kingpin when the guy asks for something to read on the toilet and his mate passes him a bottle of shampoo, and he says "New and improved. I've read this one already."

Some tall bloke who taught us time management once

Jeff Lebowsk

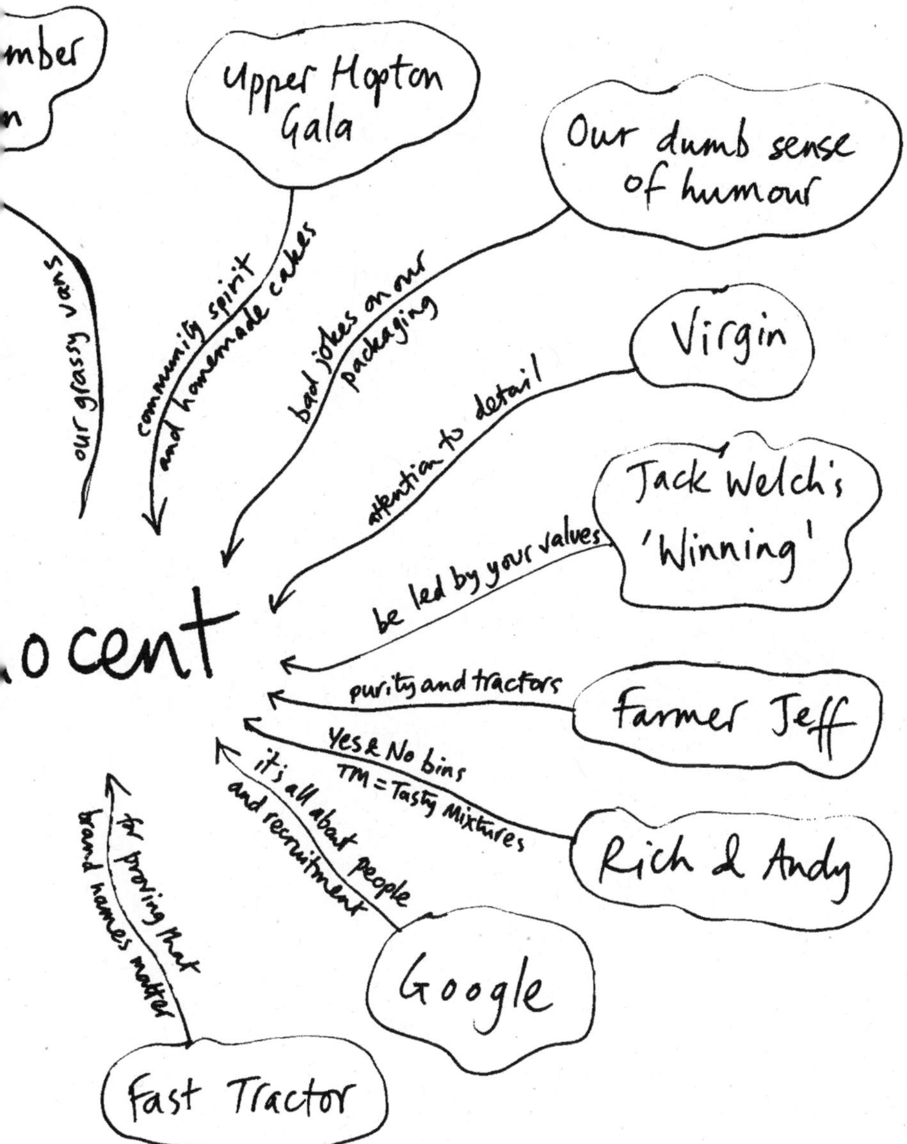

mber
n

Upper Hopton
Gala

Our dumb sense
of humour

Virgin

Jack Welch's
'Winning'

our grassy vans

community spirit
and homemade cakes

bad jokes on our
packaging

attention to detail

be led by your values

o cent

purity and tractors

Farmer Jeff

Yes & No bins

TM = Tasty Mixtures

it's all about people
and recruitment

Rich & Andy

for proving that
brand names matter

Google

Fast Tractor

MAPPING THE
INNOCENT GENOME

new pair of trousers, make sure you understand fully the process by which trousers are made – where the material comes from, how it is produced, how tailors cut the cloth, why they might choose a button over a zip. Gain a true understanding of how it all works; it will be invaluable in helping you design a fantastic pair of trousers. But never do your thinking in this 'room' as you will feel too constrained by the existing rules.

Third, visit the 'room of precedent', where you should study all that has gone before in the sector that you operate within. If you are writing an advert for a car company, look at all the ads for car companies that have ever been written. Do this to learn what has come before, what was successful and what was less so. But don't do your work in this 'room', as you will just end up plagiarising.

The final 'room' is where you should do your work. It is the 'room of creativity'. It is dark and the only person in that room is you. You should go into that room naked. And it is here that you should start to think of ideas. And if you go through the first three rooms before you get here, and make sure you listen to your own thoughts, you will have many ideas.

This is pretty much verbatim what Michael Wolff told us one time. It was quite a special moment for us all. We're not sure how useful it is, but we thought we'd put it in the book just in case it's of interest. And to explain what we're up to if we're ever found sitting in a dark room naked.

Having ideas – our golden rules

1. Leave the office

We had our big idea on holiday. You might have yours in the park while feeding the ducks, or in bed, or out walking in the country. Pretty much any place where your mind can be liberated. Your brain is hemmed in at a desk, thinking about desk things. Don't expect it to be creative when you're there.

2. Keep a notebook in your pants

Or at least keep one close by, all day and all night. Richard Branson is constantly scribbling in his, wherever he is. And we find that it's particularly useful on the bedside table – great thoughts often come to you just before you fall asleep, and if you don't write them down they're gone in the morning.

3. Start from different places

When we're trying to develop an idea for something, say a piece of packaging, we force ourselves to go wide before we go deep. In other words, it's better to come up with four completely different ways of solving the same problem before spending time working on different versions of the same basic idea. And it stops you from deciding on the solution before you've had a chance to look at the alternatives.

4. Sit in a dark room naked

It's got to be worth a try.

make money, and...

Make money, and...

Capitalism. The money-making machine that exerts its influence over every aspect of society. The mechanism by which we get our food, find shelter and buy special hats for weddings. When it comes to the way the world works, even in this post credit-crunch era, capitalism is still the biggest game in town.

The epic influence of capitalism, and its agent – the corporation – causes some to resent business. But to be anti-business ignores the fundamental contribution the world of commerce makes to the way we live. Business, for all its issues, is the sole economic engine of society. Every pound a government spends on schools, hospitals or roads has been generated by business. And every penny a charity gives to its causes will have originally come from the machine in some way. Ultimately, it is the miracle of modern consumerism itself that deserves the credit for the fact that our life expectancy has increased exponentially and our teeth have stopped falling out. That's why at innocent we are proud to be a business and keen to create as much growth, opportunity and value as we can.

That said, capitalism does have its flaws, and they're big ones. The financial meltdown of 2008 showed the fallibility of the system. The industrialisation of the world's modern economies has resulted in unprecedented environmental consequences. And as a system for distributing wealth, capitalism is unbalanced; over the last thirty years, the 33 poorest countries in the world have got poorer in absolute terms. In Africa, the young still die from malnutrition, while in America, children currently being born are thought to be the first generation (born outside of wartime) to have life expectancies shorter than their parents, mainly as a result of obesity. In other words, on Planet Earth today, there are people dying from having too much while others die from having too little. On a distant planet right now there's an intelligent alien life form looking down at us saying, 'These people really don't get it, do they?'

We believe that while capitalism has helped create this mess, it can, and must, help clean it up. We need businesses to first and foremost create wealth and fund the progress of our societies. But additionally, businesses are in a unique position to make a massive, immediate difference beyond the financial. Companies have unimaginable resources at their disposal, in the form of money, time, expertise, people and technology. In the words of Michael Lee-Porter (one of the world's most respected business thinkers), *'if after achieving its financial aims a business focuses the resources it has at its disposal, it can have a greater impact on social good than any other institution or philanthropic organisation.'* Basically his view is that a business should firstly fulfil its role in society by generating money, but after that contribute in other ways too. It should make money, and...

A compelling example of a company applying their core skills and doing this is Microsoft during the Kosovo refugee crisis of 1999. Employees in the local office recognised there was a humanitarian issue brewing when 500,000 Kosovans were displaced from their war-torn country, with no identity papers and no way of proving who they were. After speaking to the NGOs in the refugee camps, and understanding the nature of the issue, Microsoft realised there was essentially a database problem.

Volunteer software engineers from Microsoft developed and coded a mobile refugee registration system, set up tents in the camps, and used the technology to help the refugees establish their identities, contact their families and gain access to health care and other services. Since then, that same software has been used in similar refugee situations around the world, helping literally millions of displaced people to be reunited with their families and homelands. Not bad going for a bunch of geeks.

At innocent, we're still a long way from being the business we want to be in this regard. But from the outset we have worked to ensure that we leave behind a positive social and environmental legacy. We strive to leave things a little bit better than we find them, an aim that makes us sound like Miss World contestants, but a desire that is sincere nonetheless.

Rather than being just a nice-sounding proposition, our business has a specific five-point strategy to ensure we contribute positively and leave behind a legacy we can be proud of.

Leaving a better legacy – our five-point plan

1. Make it healthy

As a food company, our primary responsibility is to only ever make products that are genuinely good for people. Food and drink from innocent will always be nutritionally net-positive for those who consume it. Most food sold with logos on the front of it can't necessarily make the same claim, but innocent will never sell 'empty calorie' food or stuff that isn't naturally good for you. Our mission is to get natural, healthy food and drinks to as many people as possible.

2. Use responsible ingredients

innocent gets through a lot of fruit these days, and we want to be proud of every piece we use. So we pay a premium for fruit from farms with higher ethical accreditations that protect the rights of their workers and the local biodiversity. Our 'innocent minimum standards', which our suppliers comply with, are some of the toughest in the world in terms of protecting social and environmental standards. And our Get Closer to the Fruit team (our sustainability and quality people) make regular visits to the farms to make sure things are as they should be.

In addition to seeking out the better grown fruit, we also fund NGOs such as the Rainforest Alliance who teach farmers out in the field (literally) a more enlightened way of growing, meaning that we help to increase the supply of responsibly grown fruit in the world. Working with them, we brought the first Rainforest Alliance bananas to the UK and the first ever Rainforest Alliance pineapple juice.

We're not as good as we want to be in this area, but over the last few years we have made some important steps towards our goal of sustainability. It's one of the things that people at innocent really care about.

3. Develop sustainable packaging

The third area we push hard on is developing more environmentally conscious packaging. When we first started the company, we didn't think about the impact of our packaging – we were just happy to have bottles to put our smoothies in. But as our business grew we began to think, 'Where do all these bottles come from and where do they go?'

When we learnt that plastic is made from oil, and that most used bottles go to landfill, we began to investigate having a bottle made entirely from recycled plastic. The manufacturers told us that 100% recycled wasn't possible (the technology didn't exist to make it happen) but they could offer a 25% recycled bottle, which we accepted because at least it was a start. Then in 2006, after regular hassling, testing and stalking, we got the recycled content up to 50%.

After another 18 months of tests and research, we got to the full quota in 2007 with the resulting 100% recycled bottle delivering a 55% carbon reduction, saving over 1000 tonnes of CO_2 every year. A big step for a little company, and one we were proud of. And another example of the benefit of starting small.

We've applied the same principle of 'reduce the impact' to our other packaging formats. Our kids' wedges now use less cardboard than standard ones, and 100% of that cardboard now comes from FSC-accredited sources – the Greenpeace standard for paper and wood based products. We're getting there on our bigger cartons too: we're currently at 54% FSC and on track to get to 100%.

It's something we care about because it seems stupid not to, and because other good things may come from it. As Mike Childs, Head of Campaigns at Friends of the Earth, said, 'innocent are leading the field in their pioneering work [on recycled plastic bottles], which will hopefully be followed by others.' Thanks, Mike, we hope so too.

4. Become a resource-efficient business

Like any smart business, we try to tidy up after ourselves and stay resource-efficient. We don't want to emit any more waste or emissions than are absolutely necessary.

Our first focus has been to reduce our carbon footprint. We measure the carbon embedded in our entire business system – from the field to the fridge to the recycling bin. As you can imagine, calculating a carbon footprint for the whole business system is a complicated piece of work. But the information is critical in showing where reductions can be made, which we can then act on.

We've always used green electricity to power Fruit Towers, but the carbon audit allowed us to show our suppliers the benefit of their turning to green power too. Our most immediate success was convincing our biggest manufacturing partner to convert to green electricity, which instantly took out 15% of the CO_2 embedded in each and every innocent smoothie carton. A real, material change.

A smaller but still notable improvement was changing the way we stack our smoothies on pallets before they are put into vans to be delivered. Previously we used to stack our pallets eight layers high, which was just how it was always done. Then someone suggested stacking them ten layers high, meaning fewer pallets overall and fewer road miles, saving us 50,000 tons of CO_2 per annum and some cash in the process.

That's one of the great things about taking sustainability seriously – a lot of the time, when you're driving down waste and emissions, you're also driving down costs. So everyone's a winner.

5. Share the profits

Finally, we give a minimum of 10% of our profits to charity each year, to aid rural development projects in the countries our fruit comes from. This helps ensure that those people who need cash more than us receive some of it. Giving 10% away is a significant part of our profits, but it means we keep 90%, and our rationale is that if you can't achieve what you need to achieve in your business with 90% of your profits, then you're probably not being as efficient as you could be.

As the business has got bigger, our donations to charity have increased. To ensure the money goes to the most worthwhile places we set up a separate registered charity in 2004 called the innocent foundation, to professionally manage the donations. The foundation's aim is 'to help subsistence communities on their path to sustainable development' and it has got a track record of funding NGOs that help some of the poorest rural communities in the world, helping people get out of the grind of poverty.

To be honest, it all sounds a bit worthy. But we can live with that. Relative to our size we are one of the biggest corporate charity donors in the country, and we've seen at first hand the impact that our donations are having on rural communities. Plus, it gives our team an opportunity to help out too, as the business offers innocent foundation scholarships for members of the team to go out to work with an NGO for a fortnight, transferring their skills and getting stuck in (find out more in a couple of pages).

The projects we support

We give away 10% of our profits to charity, with most of that money going to our own separately registered innocent foundation. Here are some of the NGOs that our foundation works with:

Find Your Feet – India
Our funding has enabled FYF India to start working on a pilot project supporting 4000 adivasi (tribal) women to train in sustainable farming practices.

FARM Africa – Southern Sudan
We have agreed four years of funding to support FARM Africa's Southern Sudan Livelihoods Recovery and Development Project, focusing on subsistence agriculture.

Practical Action – Bangladesh
Our funding is supporting two Rural Technology Centres, helping 7500 farming families to build their skills and overcome the regular risk of malnutrition.

War On Want – Brazil
Our funding is aimed at helping rural labourers reduce their current dependency on exploitative middlemen, by providing basic equipment to process their own harvest.

Kaloko Trust – Zambia
We fund a three-year project that is training and equipping 150 new beekeepers as well as building the capacity of the local cooperative to support local bee-farmers and market their produce.

CARE International – Ecuador
We're helping local prickly pear producers obtain a fair price for their crops, which has historically proved a difficult thing to achieve.

Find Your Feet – India

Practical Action – Bangladesh

FARM Africa – Southern Sudan

Kaloko Trust – Zambia

War On Want – Brazil

CARE International – Ecuador

The Foundation Scholarship Programme

Helen in India: Our Helen travelled to India in 2007 to work with WOMANKIND Worldwide's partner organisation, the Irula Tribal Women's Welfare Society, where she worked with the team and redesigned their website.

Andrew in Malawi: In 2008 Andrew went to help out with the Microloan Foundation in Malawi. He worked on a project that we support via Microloan – a juice-making business that needed external business advice and help with a simple, effective business plan. Andrew was eminently qualified to help.

JT in Kenya: 2009 saw JT go to Kenya to work with an NGO called Excellent Development. We are supporting their work with farmers, helping to improve their water supply and food production. He spent time setting up a computer network for their office in the town of Kola.

Our Helen with (L to R) Peter, Bobbi, Devi and Lakshmi from the charity ITWWS

Andrew dancing with women from the Chigwirizano juice co-operative

Eunice, Ruth, Philisia and Andrew, members of the Meka self-help group, standing on one of their sand dams with JT

A slightly bigger thought

The things that society deems acceptable change over time. Two hundred years ago it was socially acceptable to be in the business of slavery. It sure isn't now. Consequently, there is a risk that in two hundred years' time, people are going to look back and say, 'Right, so you knew about all these problems – climate change, poverty in Africa, human rights abuse, war-driven humanitarian crises – and with all the money, time and resources that your business had, all you did was sell frozen pizzas?'

Not that we've got anything against frozen pizzas; they taste nice, make a valid contribution to society, and produce an economic benefit via the making and selling of them. But maybe with the pizza we can get something on the side. Bearing in mind our skills as manufacturers and marketers, our knowledge of social trends, the relationships we have with consumers and the resources at our command, maybe we can also do a bit more. Yes, as business people we must first make sure we are delivering the money, but ultimately after that can't we think of delivering Money And...?

chapter ten
listen up, open up

Listen up, open up

We love our consumers. Without them, we'd just have a very expensive hobby and a large pile of fruit out the back. As such, we want to know what our drinkers are thinking. We want to know what we can do to make ourselves a better company for them. So we do everything we can to keep a dialogue going. To proactively find ways to ask them questions, and hear what they have to say. The answers allow us to spot trends, point us in the right direction and occasionally give us a kick up the backside.

Our door is always open

We like to interact. In fact, interact is a bit of an overused term in the world of business. So what we really mean is that we like to meet people. In person. Shake hands, put the kettle on, have a chat. So on our very first labels, and to this day, we invite people to pop in if they're passing. To be honest, there's no particular agenda. People knock on the door, come in, receive the official tour, have a natter, a drink and have their photo taken for posterity, to be displayed in the official Visitors' Book.

We have had some excellent visitors over the years. We hosted an 80th birthday party for one of our drinkers (a lovely man called David Dare who is sadly no longer with us), we've had plenty of interested school kids nosing about, a man called Carlos who read out very long poems in front of the whole business and Barry, who has the innocent logo tattooed on his arm and visits regularly to check that we're still behaving ourselves. Probably the best of the bunch was a man who slept outside in his van for three nights, insisting that he could take us to a place where magic blueberries grew. It sounded tempting but we couldn't spare the time.

We like to listen

These days, we do a lot of our listening on the web. We've always tried to make our website as open and conversational as possible, and we keep evolving it, adding tools and features as we think of them. One of its most useful features is its 'rate and review' function, where drinkers can comment on our recipes. They tell us what's tasting great, what they're bored of and what they'd like us to do next. Over the years, the single biggest request we've had (via rate and review, email, Twitter, blog, phone, letter, etc) is for us to make a banana-free smoothie. So having listened to this, we've finally perfected a recipe that is bereft of bananas (it should be in the shops by the time you're reading this).

Without having all of those open channels via which people could tell us what they wanted, we probably wouldn't have made the recipe. Adding the rate and review function of our site meant we were giving people a dedicated place to tell us exactly what they want, and giving ourselves a mandate to act upon popular requests. Smoothies by the people, for the people.

Then there's our blog. Blogging has encouraged us to stay focused on our drinkers. The blog is just another space in which we ask questions, suggest new ideas and then listen to what people think. Launching our Veg Pots in 2008 was the culmination of endless nights dreaming of vegetables in all their glory and wondering how we could get people to eat more of them. And although it's still early days, the Veg Pots are doing well.

But there was one reaction that we hadn't foreseen, from a vocal group of people who we met on the blog. Vegans, who we had thought would be in the group of people who might enjoy our Veg Pots more than most, started posting complaints about the presence of honey in a couple of the Veg Pots – since honey comes from bees, vegans couldn't consume a Veg Pot. In direct response to this feedback we went back into the kitchen, played with the recipes and got them tasting spot on without the use of honey. We redeveloped a new range just after launch purely as a result of access to information that, as non-vegans, we hadn't known. Just by being porous and by listening, we turned a negative into a product improvement.

innocent
little tasty drinks

things we make   us

daily thoughts
weekly news

thought for food

Dr Shilpee
talks health

daily thoughts

This is what's on our mind today.
If you fancy getting a weekly digest in your inbox, join the family here

« monday makes you get it wrong | Main | let us pray »

January 28, 2008

how many people can you fit in the post room?

this is the post room

...to see how many people we could fit in...

innocent
little tasty drinks

things we make   us   (news)   family   bo

daily thoughts
weekly news

thought for food

Dr Shilpee
talks health

save pounds

where to find our best
value smoothies

new
special
guest

pineapples,
blueberries
& ginger

oranges: the centre of our universe

say hello to our new
orange juice

say hello to our new veg pots

one tasty
meal, three
portions
of veg

daily thoughts

This is what's on our mind today.
If you fancy getting a **weekly digest** in your inbox, join the family here

« you won the pants | Main | in danish »

October 10, 2006

strides

Matt's trousers - wise move or not? Is the half tartan thing cutting it? You decide.

Posted by dan on October 10, 2006 at 11:21 PM in **our people** | Permalink

Technorati Tags: **trousers**

recent comments
Celia on n...
Row...

Hot stuff.

I've just noticed that we've got giant red chilli winged smoke detectors in the rafters of
...te sprinklers?

innocent
little tasty drinks

things we make   us   news   family   bored?   press

daily thoughts
weekly news

thought for food

Dr Shilpee
talks health

save pounds

where to find our best
value smoothies

new
special guest

pineapples,
blueberries
& ginger

oranges: the centre of our universe
say hello to our new
orange juice

say hello to our new veg pots

one tasty
meal, three
portions
of veg

visit our FaceBook page
facebook

daily thoughts

This is what's on our mind today.
If you fancy getting a **weekly digest** in your inbox, join the family **here**

January 23, 2008

getting to the bottom of things

Fancy writing something funny to go on the bottom of our bottles?

Yes? Great. Here's the rules.

- Messages must be 40 characters or less.
- Spaces, hyphens, apostrophes and stuff all count as a character.
- Leave your entry as a comment to this blog post.
- Fill in the email bit when you leave a comment so that we can get in contact with you if you win.
- As many entries per person as you like.
- Extra points for making us laugh.
- Our 3 favourites will be used on millions of bottles across the land, something to tell the grandkids.
- We'll send the 3 winners lots of smoothies too.
- The deadline is Midnight on Thursday 24th January.
- So be quick.

Update:
We've just chosen the winners and the standard was so high we ended up choosing 7 instead of 3. You can see who won and find out a bit more about their authors by **clicking here with your mouse**.

A big thank you to everyone who took the time to enter. We hope you enjoyed thinking up the messages as much as we enjoyed reading them.

Posted by ted on January 23, 2008 at 09:28 AM in **help** | **Permalink** |
Comments (1594) | **TrackBack (0)**

January 21, 2008

subscribe to this blog's fe[ed]

recent comments
Celia on **new employee**
Rowan on **blind cheese**
stevo on **blind cheese**
Christine Evans on **time flies**
Cazzoo on the **loo of love**
Isabelle on **master chef (sor**
ted at innocent on **mastherche**
finals (sort of)
natalie on **hands off**
Sam on **masterchef semi fi**
of)
Lydia on **ukulele idol**

some other stuff by us
twitter
our twitter feed
- @elspethjardy *It blinks*
ago
- @ynzo *well hello Ynzo, w*
you amongst the 507 new
all's well in the 'dam. about
- *doing another load of fol*
believe another 507 people
follow us in the last 7 days
507 new people. about 22

You Tube
our YouTube channel

facebook
our FaceBook page

flickr
our big knit 2008 flickr
our veg pot veg art flie
our 2008 village fete fl
our 2008 AGM flickr g

our other blogs
innocent in Sweden b
innocent in Ireland b
innocent in Denmark
our Big Knit 'knitter-
our innocent village
*contains foreign language

recent posts
flip masters
an update from mal
blind cheese
ukulele idol
whether you're a b
you're a mother
healthy teens

Martin the magician and his magic hands

visit our FaceBook page
facebook

We use these wild blueberries, which are
ones you'll find in the

The banana phone

We're always contactable by phone. Most companies use this as a complaints forum and as a result 'customer relations' almost always has slightly negative connotations. We prefer to use the phone as BT intended, as a way to stay in touch.

The original banana phone was purchased at Woolworths (RIP) near our first office in Ladbroke Grove around the time of our launch as a bit of a joke. It was our main office phone – the phone that rang whether it was a distributor ordering drinks, or a drinker wanting to ask a question about our recipes. We put the number on the labels and started answering every call with a cheery 'Hello, innocent banana phone', mainly because it was a phone that looked like a banana and it made us laugh.

We didn't expect this to become a hallowed tradition. But to this day, if that number rings at Fruit Towers, whoever answers will trill a cheery 'Hello, innocent banana phone', even though the phone on their desk is probably grey injection-moulded plastic (the original banana phone is far too valuable to be used as a mere phone and has its own special velvet cushion and plinth).

The banana phone is special, because everyone still answers it. We want everyone to be part of the amorphous permeable blob we mentioned earlier. So although Rowena and Joe (our People's Champions, tasked with making our drinkers happy beyond belief) usually pick it up first, if they don't get to it in the first three rings every phone in the office will ring, meaning that anyone could pick it up. It could be with regard to praise, a minor complaint, or just someone wanting to tell us about their holidays. But since anyone in any part of our business could end up having a chat with our drinkers, it brings every member of our business closer to our customers and reminds them of the reason why and ultimately for whom they are doing their jobs. We're also in a much better position to answer questions relating to innocent than a generic call centre could ever be.

Fruitstock and the Village Fete

We like to meet the people who drink our drinks. Adam didn't have enough chairs at his house to host a dinner party for 2 million people so we came up with the idea of Fruitstock, a free music festival in Regent's Park. It would be a bigger version of the music festival we organised when we did our YES and NO bin test. It would also be an event that would cost us hundreds of thousands of pounds to organise, with no guarantee that anyone would turn up. A truly excellent idea. At best it would be a chance for us to gauge the level of interest in our brand, and at worst we'd have the park to ourselves for a day.

Relying on the *Field of Dreams* premise, 'If you build it, they will come', we sat and waited for people to turn up. And they did. People came because they liked the drinks, and they told their friends to come too. We didn't really spend any money advertising it – we just wrote about it on the bottle labels and hoped that word would get around. Word did and we had about 30,000 attending in 2003, rising to over 150,000 in 2006, which is when the sheer volume of people got slightly scary and we decided to replace Fruitstock with a more family orientated, intimate event.

So in 2007 the innocent village fete was born. Based upon the Upper Hopton Gala (a key event in Richard's Yorkshire upbringing), our fete involved cream teas, Morris dancing, ferret racing and dog agility displays. And as well as all of those traditional fete fixtures, we added a bit of live music, a DJ tent, a poetry café, the innocent kissing parlour, ballroom dancing lessons and plenty of posh food and drink.

In common with Fruitstock, the most important thing about the fete is having the chance to meet our customers. Prior to these weekends we remind each other that this is our big chance to meet the real boss: the people who ultimately pay our wages and keep us in a job. So we always strive to make the best impression possible. Hair is combed, shirts are tucked in and we make sure we're all over the festival site, helping out as much as we can. We wear T-shirts saying 'Hello. I work at innocent. Fancy a chat?' making it crystal clear who we are and why we're there.

If people want to find out more about us, they can visit the 'come and say hello area' (between the cider tent and the duck herding), where people from each key area of our business (from HR to sustainability to operations to recipe inventing) are available to answer questions and chat about what we do. We've had to make this bit bigger every year as it gets swamped, and it's where people also give us their thoughts on our adverts, our packaging and the new recipes that we're testing out right there and then.

Which leads us to consumer research...

Asking questions

The traditional way of finding out what consumers think is to have focus groups on particular subjects. This normally involves finding 12 people from a particular demographic and sticking them in a room with some free buns. Then someone clever fires complicated questions at them for an hour and a half. This process has its place, but the downside is that the results can be misleading. The groups are small, and therefore not entirely representative of the target market. And it's ultimately artificial – people wouldn't normally consider the relative crispiness of different types of cornflake for quite that long, or in quite that detail. The lure of free biscuits and the opportunity to maybe watch an advert or two may keep them committed for a short time, but focus groups often lack focus from the group. The tendency is to end up agreeing with everything the interrogators are asking, with little differentiation in opinion.

We still undertake the odd focus group when necessary, but we strongly believe that the best way in which to get compelling answers to your questions is through forums which engage and interest your audience, such as...

Our weekly newsletter and the blog

We talk about the genesis of the innocent family and our newsletter on page 129. We've nurtured a friendly and interactive relationship with the people comprising the innocent family, which means we can use the newsletter and this amazing contact list to ask certain important questions and to glean information if people want to join in.

We've shown them potential adverts and asked for their views, with their answers directly influencing whether those ads have run. We've asked them whether we should sell our smoothies in McDonald's – a big, controversial decision that elicited some strong views from the off. The size of the group and the form of the communication means that we can get a general view from a large sample size and also have the facility to really nail down the concerns of smaller groups (and individuals) who hold particularly strong views either way.

In 2006 we started blogging, which seemed like a natural extension of our weekly news efforts, with the added benefit that people could immediately post their thoughts and comments about anything we were up to. It's a place where we stow our collective thinking and give our drinkers the opportunity to say what's on their minds.

A small example of how it has worked beautifully was when in 2008 we posted a small request, asking people to submit lines that would end up being embossed on the bottoms of our bottles. We'd been hiding random pearls of wisdom there for years, ever since we'd realised that as we had our own proprietary mould for our bottles, we could write whatever we wanted. We didn't tell anyone they were there, but occasionally someone would excitedly phone or email us to say they'd found the secret message, which was usually a variation upon the classic 'Please stop looking at my bottom' (took us ages to come up with that).

After our limited supply of bottom gags eventually dwindled we turned to our drinkers for help (see page 181). We thought a few people might post an idea, but after a couple of days the count was over

1500, and they were good too – much better than ours. In the end we chose all seven of the new bottom lines from those posted by drinkers, and 'Trapped in bottle factory – send help' might well go down as the best ever. In fact, because our drinkers had done the work for us, the additional benefit was that we could focus on other things. One of those in fact being the innocent AGM.

The innocent AGM

Our AGM was the natural culmination of lots of the things that came before it – our festivals, the story of the YES/NO bins, our weekly email news, the blog and our 'knock on the door' policy. In 2008 it seemed about time to get some serious, in-depth face time with those very important people – the drinkers.

So we invited the innocent family (all 120,000 of them) to take part in a ballot in order to obtain one of 100 places. The AGM took place on a Saturday, with people travelling from all over the UK to come to Fruit Towers, where we had structured sessions on all aspects of the business – making the perfect smoothie, designing packaging, how our innocent foundation works, etc. After people had learnt and told us what they thought in smaller groups, we held a lengthy Q&A session with the founders, with plenty of tea and cake thrown in for good measure.

What we got out of that day was immeasurable. Sure, there were material responses from people about which recipes they wanted us to make next, and how they thought we could run the business better, but more importantly it encouraged an underlying feeling of humility on our part. However smart we think we are, however much success our business has, we are in the hands of those people, and it pays well for us to shut up and listen to what they have to say.

Get people engaged

We consider active participation another important facet of maintaining a good relationship with our customers. One of the best examples of this is the Big Knit. It has been mentioned elsewhere in this book, but in a nutshell, in 2004 a man called New Adam (who worked in our marketing team) came up with the idea of putting little woolly hats on our bottles in shops. Each one sold would raise 50p for Age Concern, to help keep older people warm during winter.

But who would knit the hats? Well, New Adam managed to get our drinkers and old people's groups involved – a virtuous altruistic loop was born, with old people knitting furiously, sending the hats to us, and then benefiting themselves from the money raised. Without our consumers' participation, this project would never have got off the ground. But with their help, it raised over a quarter of a million pounds in 2008.

We'd love to find another idea that's that good, so if you think you've got such an idea, email it to thenextbigthing@innocentdrinks.com. One thing's for sure about good ideas – you never know where they're going to come from. No reason why it shouldn't be you.

The atypical consumer

Some of our customers are real fans of the brand. A small number of them take their passion very seriously indeed, and we encourage them to express themselves in whatever way they see fit. Some, like Barry, have had the 'dude' logo tattooed permanently upon their person; others have outdone themselves in a creative capacity and crafted shoes out of innocent cartons. Others lovingly bake exquisite pastries and cakes to feed us with. We received 39 homemade birthday cakes on our 6th birthday and every single one of them was polished off before teatime.

One lady called Caroline Nash even sent us a small tapestry that she'd made, featuring our logo against a pretty stitched background.

It became famous throughout the office. People started rubbing it for good luck. It became known as 'The Tapestry'. Richard had a spell of carrying it around with him wherever he went, like some holy relic, showing it to whoever he met, claiming that it was the essence of all that innocent should be – spontaneous, unsolicited, natural, homemade, etc.

To look at it you'd think it was an old piece of cloth. But it was and still is much more than that. It is…The Tapestry.

Some innocent drinkers who've been in touch along the way...

| Barry and his tattoo | Kev's mum with her innocent shoes | Richard in his hot air balloon |

The Tapestry, by Caroline Nash

It's not just about consumers

Of course, its not just our drinkers that we need to pay attention to. We simply could not produce our smoothies without the help of everyone at every stage in our supply chain – from suppliers and manufacturers to distributors and retailers. We need a constant dialogue with these people too. We draft a bi-annual survey to get their comments on our systems and to work out where we need to improve. In a spirit of transparency and openness we invite our retailers to see our kitchens so they can understand our processes and how we work. In turn we study and discuss their business plans and annual goals so we can assess how best to help them deliver their objectives.

We believe we need to look at the supply chain as a whole. So we're keen to persuade people to buy into the same vision that we have. To that end we give regular talks to our suppliers about sustainability, and our main supplier was so convinced by the arguments that they signed up to 100% green electricity. We hold regular parties and smaller events for those that help make us tick, and they are always invited to our VNP (very nice person) tent at Fruitstock/the Village Fete, where they are wined, dined and massaged to within an inch of their lives.

Keep listening

This is probably the longest chapter in the book, but that's because it's very important. Businesses that don't listen end up failing. So all we would say is that in order to gather information from the people who make your business tick (your customers), you need to stay in touch and put out as many feelers and sensors as you can. Wiretap your target market. Everything you do should suggest an attitude of availability and a willingness to listen. Each and every method is valuable, even the less engaging and more traditional ones, because taken together they give you access to the minds of the people that are buying your product.

Some of the things people have sent us. Letters, photos, bespoke needlework...

Once you have this information you need to filter and condense it. Interpret the data and the emotions to decode the true underlying need. This is obviously very important – Henry Ford once commented that if he had made what his consumers actually asked for he would have built a faster horse. So listen to everything but be smart about what it's telling you. And find the nuggets of pure gold that you can realistically action.

Finally, remember that through the process of listening, consumers can and always will remind you of the main thing that you should be focusing on, the thing that is most important to them. See opposite for our favourite example.

If you ever fancy getting in touch with us, please feel free to call the banana phone on 020 8600 3993, email hello@innocentdrinks.com or pop in to Fruit Towers if you're passing. There's a drink here with your name on it.

dear Captain
My name is Nicola im 8
years. old. this is my first
flight but im not scared. I
like to watch the clouds go
by. My mum says the crew is
nice. I think your plane is
good. thanks for a nice flight
don't fuck up the landing
           Luv Nicola 
                     Xx xx

A letter written by an 8-year-old girl on a
Quantas flight to be given to the pilot of the
plane. The best example we've seen of a
consumer reminding someone of the main thing.

an innocent timeline

1998

Rich, Adam and Jon decide to start a business, and write the business plan (12 different versions).

1999

The first innocent smoothie is sold at Out To Lunch on Conlan Street, London W10.

2000

innocent launches yoghurt thickies. Nobody notices.

1998

They meet Mr Pinto, who invests at the last minute.

1999

The workforce doubles to six.

2000

innocent arrives in Ireland.

2001

The Manchester office opens (Paul's bedroom).

2002

We write our first recipe book (*Little book of drinks*).

2003

We launch the first ever big smoothies (750ml bottles) and Juicy Waters.

2001

Caroline Nash sends us The Tapestry.

2002

We buy our first electric car. Our first electric car breaks down.

2003

The first Fruitstock happens in Regent's Park, London.

an innocent timeline

2004

We write our second book (*Stay Healthy, Be Lazy*) and launch Super Smoothies, featuring the first ever carrot smoothie.

2005

We test out innocent ice cream at Fruitstock 05.

2006

Two men and a camcorder make the first innocent TV ad in Gunnersbury Park and our 100th person joins us (Heather).

2004

innocent opens for business in France, Holland and Belgium and we launch Supergran (later to become The Big Knit).

2005

innocent smoothies for kids launch at Brackenbury Primary school (across the road).

2006

We write a new book and call it the *innocent smoothie recipe book*. We start blogging and Mike says it'll never catch on.

2007

We launch our breakfast thickie (featuring oats), start using goji berries and get burgled.

2008

We hold our first ever AGM, launch orange juice properly (in big cartons) and we branch out into veg with the launch of tasty veg pots.

2009

We celebrate ten years in business and get this book finished.

2007

Bunting fever grips us as the first ever innocent village fete happens, we open for business in Germany, Sweden and Austria and our 200th person joins (Sally).

2008

Daisy, the first lady of Fruit Towers, leaves us (sob). And it rains at the second village fete. But spirits are not dampened.

2009

And we invent a couple of things that we can't tell you about yet...

Thank you

To anyone who has ever drunk one of our drinks. We couldn't do it without you.

To all of the retailers who buy and sell our drinks. We salute you.

To all of the people who have worked at innocent, past and present. You are the business.

To the farmers, growers and suppliers who we work with. Thank you for making innocent possible.

To the journalists who have written about us and helped us get noticed.

To Maurice for believing in us in the first place so we could get started.

To our parents, friends and countless other people who have offered help and advice along the way.

And to Jose, our office cleaner – the hardest working man in fruit juice.

Credits

Words
Richard Reed
Dan Germain

Design
Kat Linger

Watchful eye
Tansy Drake
Melinda Reed

Illustration
Ben Williams
Dan Germain

Photography
Mark Read
The innocent archives

Editors
Kate Adams
Laura Herring

Please come to our first birthday party

Dan   Jon   Rich   Adam   Bro

innocent's first birthday at a surprise venue, London W10, 8pm

PENGUIN BOOKS

Published by the Penguin Group
Penguin Books Ltd, 80 Strand, London WC2R 0RL, England
Penguin Group (USA) Inc., 375 Hudson Street, New York, New York 10014, USA
Penguin Group (Canada), 90 Eglinton Avenue East, Suite 700, Toronto, Ontario, Canada M4P 2Y3
(a division of Pearson Penguin Canada Inc.)
Penguin Ireland, 25 St Stephen's Green, Dublin 2, Ireland (a division of Penguin Books Ltd)
Penguin Group (Australia), 707 Collins Street, Melbourne, Victoria 3008, Australia
(a division of Pearson Australia Group Pty Ltd)
Penguin Random House India, 7th Floor, Infinity Tower C, DLF Cyber City, Phase - III,
Guragon (Haryana), 122 002, India
Penguin Group (NZ), 67 Apollo Drive, North Shore 0632, New Zealand
(a division of Pearson New Zealand Ltd)
Penguin Books (South Africa) (Pty) Ltd, Block D, Rosebank Office Park, 181 Jan Smuts Avenue,
Parktown North, Gauteng 2193, South Africa

Penguin Books Ltd, Registered Offices: 80 Strand, London WC2R 0RL, England

www.penguin.com

Published in Penguin Books 2009

6

Text copyright © Dan Germain and Richard Reed, 2009
All rights reserved

Page 144, left: image supplied by Cinetext/Allstar Collection

The moral right of the authors has been asserted

Printed in England by Pureprint Group

ISBN: 978-0-718-15317-5

Thanks mum